Cut the Bullshit
Land the Job:
A Guide to Resume Writing, Interviewing, Networking, LinkedIn, Salary Negotiation, and More!

Written By: Jennifer Jelliff-Russell

Cut the Bullshit Land the Job: A Guide to Resume Writing, Interviewing, Networking, LinkedIn, Salary Negotiation, and More!
by Jennifer Jelliff-Russell (Evergrowth Coach LLC)

www.EvergrowthCoach.com

For information about special discounts available for bulk purchases, sales promotions, or educational needs, contact Jennifer Jelliff-Russell at 802-676-0550 or Evergrowthcoach@gmail.com

Cover by Luigi99 from 99Designs

Ebook ISBN: 978-1-7342846-1-4

Table of Contents

Introduction   I

Identifying the Problem   IV

Tips for All Job Seekers   VI

Chapter 1: The Job Search   1
   Job Search Avenues   1
   How to Effectively Job Search (Making a Plan)   5
   Identifying Useful Keywords   7
   Am I Qualified?   8

Chapter 2: Creating or Updating a Resume   10
   The Purpose of a Resume   10
   Identifying Industry-Specific Keywords   13
   Creating a Resume from Scratch   14
   Major Sections of a Resume   15

Chapter 3: Creating a Cover Letter   36
   The Purpose of a Cover Letter   36
   How to Build a Cover Letter   39
   How to Submit a Cover Letter   42

Chapter 4: The Application Process   43
   Online Applications   43
   I've Applied, Now What?   48

Chapter 5: Networking   51
   Who Do You Network With?   52
   Different Types of Networking   52
   Acing the Networking Event (and Building an Elevator Pitch)   53

Chapter 6: LinkedIn   58
   Creating a Professional Profile   58
   Building Connections   62
   What to Avoid on LinkedIn   65

Chapter 7: Interview Preparation   **67**

    General Interview Tips   68

    Types of Interviews   69

    Interview Do's and Don'ts   70

    Interview Practice Questions   77

    Situational Questions and The STAR Method   82

    Questions to Ask the Interviewer   85

Chapter 8: Salary Negotiation   **90**

    Setting Realistic Expectations   90

    How to Actually Negotiate   92

    Putting it All Together into an Effective Argument   95

Closing   **98**

Resources   **99**

    Job Search Resources   100

    Employment Assistance   100

    Interview Practice Resources   100

    Interview Attire Assistance   100

    Action Verbs for Resume   101

Cover Letter Examples   **102**

Resume Examples   **108**

About the Author   **151**

Introduction

"I've been applying to jobs for four months and I haven't gotten a single interview!"

"I thought I had some good interviews, but no one is calling me back with an offer."

"I just can't seem to find a job to apply for that's the right fit!"

"How am I supposed to network if I don't know anyone in my field?"

"Where do I even start with my job search?"

Any of these sound familiar? If so, then Cut the Bullshit, Land the Job is the right book for you.

This book serves two main purposes. First, it helps you determine what is holding you back in your job search process. You see, these days, the majority of job seekers like yourself will go through a lengthy process to get a job offer. It starts with the job search, and then you create a resume and cover letter before applying online for the role. After that, you'll complete at least one interview before receiving the job offer and negotiating a salary. That's a minimum of least five major steps to complete before starting a new job—which means that there are five potential steps that might trip you up and keep you from moving forward to start that new dream job!

Remember, this book is here to help you cut the bullshit from the job search process. If something you're doing in the job search process is already working for you, then there's no reason to redo that step. So, rather than make you restart your entire job search process, I've provided a handy section with a simple decision tree to help you identify what the problem is in your process. (That section is conveniently titled, "Identifying the Problem.")

Using the decision tree will allow you to jump straight to the section or step with which you need the most assistance. (However, I highly recommend all job seekers read the Tips for All Job Seekers section regardless of which step you're currently stuck on.)

For those of you who haven't started the job search process yet, you can avoid getting stuck on any of the steps by reading this book from cover to cover. An even better option would be to start at the beginning and read each section before implementing the respective steps of the job search process.

That brings me to the second purpose of this book, which is to make sure that you get all the necessary information to not only get past the step that you're currently stumped by, but also cruise through the rest of the steps in the job search process until you land that coveted dream job!

So...Is this Book Worth It?

Some of the biggest issues I've seen in books for job seekers is that they are ridiculously short, only cover one or two steps of the job search process (which means you have to buy multiple books), lack details in how to actually go about completing a step, or are merely a commercial for the author's other products or services.

Since my goal with *Cut the Bullshit, Land the Job* is to provide you with advice and suggestions to be successful in every step of the job search process, I've tried to make the book as comprehensive as possible. As long as you follow the recommendations within this book, you shouldn't need to buy other job search guides since this one covers everything!

Also, in an effort to be useful to those next-level job seekers who have the basics down for a section but want to make themselves an even more desirable candidate, I've included extra suggestions in each section labeled, "Next-Level Job Seeker." These typically appear at the end of a section or subsection.

Lastly, while I do offer coaching and employment services, this is the only time you'll hear me mention it. I will, on occasion, refer you to external, mostly free resources for more in-depth assistance and will also direct you to visit my website to download a free resume template into which you'll be able to type directly.

Only You Can Prevent...Failing a Job Search Step

It might seem obvious to say, but you are the only person in charge of your job search process. Part of cutting the bullshit during the job search process includes a little tough love and making sure that you, the job seeker, are realistic about your career goals and job expectations, and are actually willing to do the work to land the job. While there might be external factors that make it more difficult for you to get a position, you are still responsible for doing everything you can to present yourself to the employer as the best candidate possible. Why am I saying this? Because the more responsibility you decide to take right now for your job search process, the more likely you will be to land the position.

Time to Cut the Bullshit

If you're ready to make some changes to your job search strategy and take a different approach to your job search process, I'm ready to provide you with the information you need to be successful in landing the job.

Let's get started!

Identifying the Problem

If you're at the beginning of your job search process and want to start out on the right foot, go ahead and start this book by jumping into the Tips for All Job Seekers section and reading chronologically from there.

However, if you're already in the middle of a job search and are feeling stuck on a certain step, check out the decision-tree diagram below to identify what the problem is and get an idea of where to start.

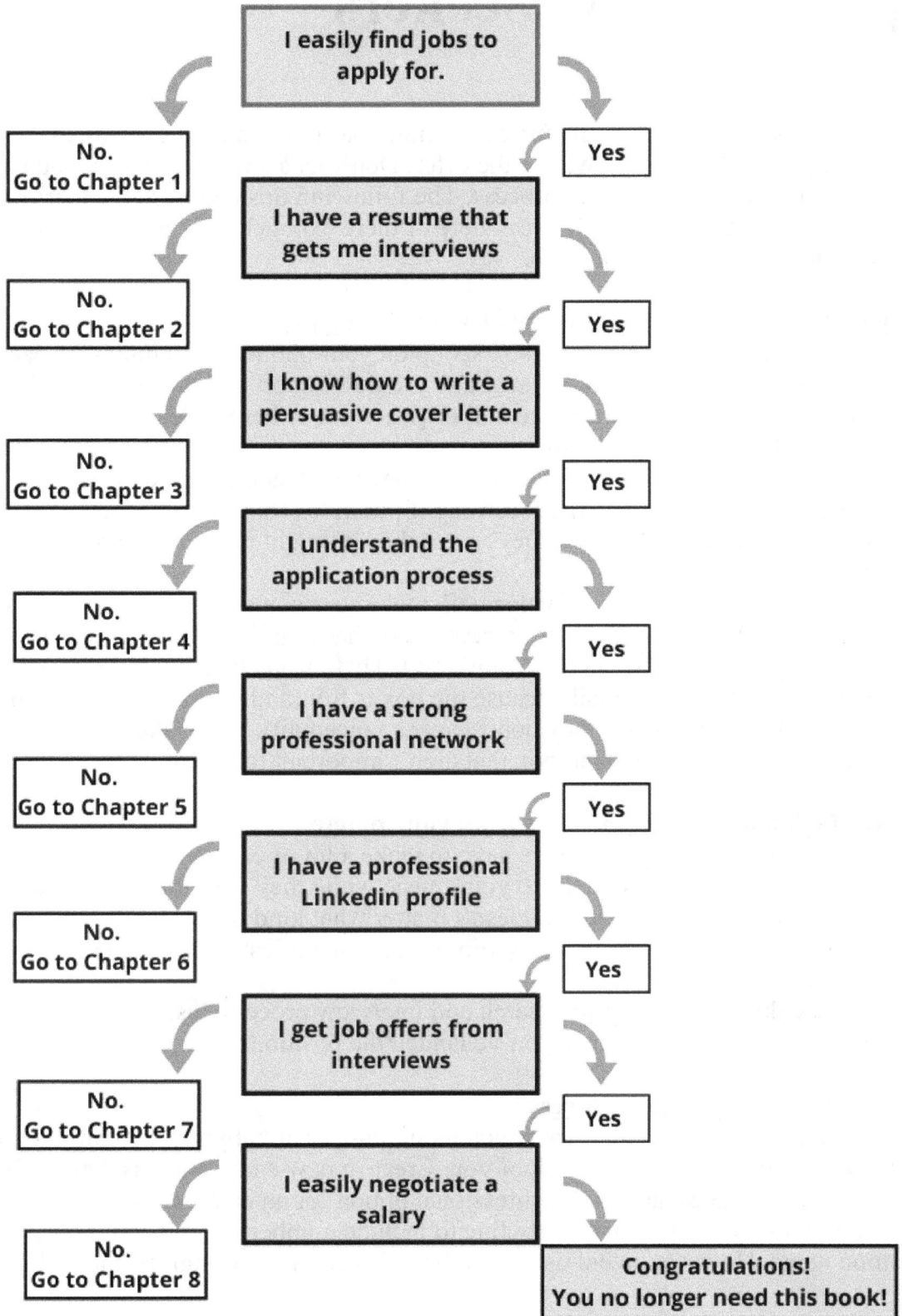

Start Here

I easily find jobs to apply for.

No. Go to Chapter 1

Yes

I have a resume that gets me interviews

No. Go to Chapter 2

Yes

I know how to write a persuasive cover letter

No. Go to Chapter 3

Yes

I understand the application process

No. Go to Chapter 4

Yes

I have a strong professional network

No. Go to Chapter 5

Yes

I have a professional Linkedin profile

No. Go to Chapter 6

Yes

I get job offers from interviews

No. Go to Chapter 7

Yes

I easily negotiate a salary

No. Go to Chapter 8

Yes

Congratulations! You no longer need this book!

Tips for All Job Seekers

No matter what step you're currently on in your job search, these tips can be helpful for making sure you make it all the way to the offer. Don't let a small issue hold you back from moving forward in your job search process. The following tips come from experiences with previous clients where just a small tweak here or there exponentially increased an employer's willingness to consider them for a job.

Set up your voicemail and create a professional greeting

If you don't have a voicemail box set up on your phone, then employers can't leave you a message to set up an interview. Your message should be short and professional. Something along the lines of, "You've reached the voicemail of [insert name here]. Please leave your name and number so that I can return your call."

If you prefer to use the prerecorded message which comes standard on your phone, make sure to at least add your name to the recording if possible. That way when employers call to schedule an interview, they'll know they've reached the right person and are more likely to bother leaving you a voicemail.

While we're on the topic of voicemail, make sure you are periodically clearing out your voicemail box of old messages. Your voicemail box has a limit of how many messages it can hold and you won't get any kind of alert when it's full. That means that employers may call you but won't be able to leave a voicemail because the box is full (and if you're like me, you'll just assume it's a telemarketer calling when they don't leave a voicemail). So go ahead right now and clear out any messages from your voicemail box that aren't important to you.

Remove playback or ringback tones from your phone

Recruiters and hiring managers have to make a lot of calls when they are trying to fill open positions. They do not want to listen to your music while they wait for you (or your now-professional voicemail) to answer. It doesn't matter what kind of music it is. Trust me when I say that recruiters will not think that you are more professional just because you've set classical music as your ringback tone.

For the duration of your job search and interview process, just disable the ringback tone. You can always set it back up once you've landed the position.

Create a professional email address

Though your friends may know you as supralover or babymama95, this is not how you want your potential employer to think of you. Create a new email address that you'll only use for the job search. The safest and most professional option for an email address will include some variation of your name. It's completely fine to include numbers on the end, especially if you have a common name. However, avoid using numbers that carry some significance (ahem, 69 or 666).

It's also a good idea to avoid using the email address provided by your current employer. Applying for a new position with the email issued by your current employer is just seen as poor etiquette. After all, why would an employer want to hire someone who clearly uses company time to apply for other jobs? While we're at it, don't use your college email address either. College email servers are usually pretty strict about the file sizes they'll accept and sometimes they'll automatically sort emails from potential employers into your junk mail folder. Also, there is a chance that after graduation, your account could be disabled (depending on your institution's policies.) You wouldn't want to lose access to the account and possibly miss out on important emails from potential employers!

Lastly, if you're still lugging around an old AOL email address, it's time to upgrade to a new email provider. Using an AOL address for a job search will likely show an employer your age and opens you up to potential discrimination. This can be especially true if you're applying for roles in the technology industry.

Do not just show up at an office and ask for a job

Though this used to be a normal practice, showing up at an office to inquire about possible job opportunities is no longer an acceptable practice for most positions (with an exception for entry-level roles in the service or restaurant industries). In today's job market, this actually makes you look a little lazy and out of sync with the times. Instead, it is expected that you will do some online research about that company to see if they have posted any positions on their website.

It is also not advisable to show up at an office, unannounced and uninvited, to follow up on a job application. Instead, wait two weeks after you apply for the position, then email or call the company's human resources department to follow up on your application.

Clean up your social media accounts or set them to "Private" mode

Today's employer is likely to look up your social media accounts before they even call you in for an interview. If you know you have unprofessional posts on Facebook, Twitter, Instagram, etc., then consider changing your settings to "Private" while you job search. Keep in mind that while this keeps those not connected to you from viewing your account, your "friends" or connections on these social media accounts will still be able to see your posts. Private mode also does not keep others from seeing your comments unless you've specifically changed the comment settings.

If you have a LinkedIn profile, then you should only ever be posting professional content on it. This means you should avoid posting anything that has to do with religion or politics. You'll get more information regarding LinkedIn by reading Chapter 6.

Be nice to everyone

Though this is a good rule to live by in general, being nice to people becomes even more important when you're applying and interviewing for positions. If you're nice to everyone, then you're unlikely to accidentally burn bridges with a company. How you treat others, especially lower-level employees, is a great indicator of your personality and how you'll act on the job. If you start out on the wrong foot—being rude to an administrative assistant who is scheduling your interview, not holding the door for the person behind you (who might turn out to be the CEO!) as you enter the building for an interview, or complaining to the company's secretary about how long the interview process is taking—you might not have the opportunity to regain respect and show what a good person and employee you can be.

Instead, try to be nice to people in general and you won't end up accidentally offending someone at your potential place of employment.

Apply to multiple positions (don't put all your eggs in one basket)

Don't apply for one role at a time and wait to hear back. This practice grossly extends the time it takes you to land a role. Unless you are only interested in leaving your current job for that specific position, then the best bet for landing a new job is to apply for multiple roles at the same time. This is a perfectly acceptable practice and could be beneficial if you end up receiving more than one job offer since you can then potentially use the situation to negotiate a higher salary (see Chapter 8 for more information on salary negotiation.)

Respect yourself

No matter how much you want a job, it's not worth it if the employer treats you poorly. While it's great to be nice to everyone, that doesn't mean you have to debase yourself or jump through ridiculous hoops to get a job. If someone treats you poorly during the hiring or interview process, don't brush it off. These are red flags that could be an indicator of what's to come if you take the role.

If you really want the position but aren't getting a good feeling during the interview process, see if you can find a connection on LinkedIn who previously worked for that company. Message them and let them know you're considering a role at that organization but wanted to get a better feel for that company before moving forward. They may be willing to give you feedback on their experience with that organization and are less likely to be biased since they no longer work there.

Chapter 1
The Job Search

When searching for a new position, one of the most integral yet difficult steps of the job search is the very first one: the actual process of searching for positions. In the age of the internet with hundreds if not thousands of websites dedicated solely to connecting job seekers like yourself with potential positions, you would think that the job search would be easier. Unfortunately, having so many job search websites from which to choose has actually muddied the waters and usually only leaves you with more questions like: Should you sign up for all the free job search websites? Are paid job boards worth it? How do you effectively job search for a niche position?

In this section, I'll address those questions and others that you might encounter. I'll also provide suggestions for how to deal with job search burnout and detail the most effective method for the job search process.

Job Search Avenues

While the classified section of newspapers still exists (mostly online,) you're less likely to see employers posting their positions through this medium as it doesn't reach as wide an audience as it once did. Instead, most employers now post their open positions on job search websites, local job boards, networking sites like LinkedIn, and/or solely their own company's career website.

Company Websites

The vast majority of organizations, companies, and businesses have their own website, and many post their open positions there. If there is a particular company for which you'd like to work, run a quick general online search by typing in the name of the company and then the word "careers." If that particular company has a web page with a list of their open positions, it should be one of the options generated by your search. Once you've found the right website, you should be able to look at their list of open positions. Bookmark these career sites so that you can occasionally check back for newly posted positions.

The downside of this job search method is that it's very time consuming and requires you to frequently check the site to see if any new positions have been posted. Plus, if you only use this method, then you'll miss out on seeing positions at other companies with which you might not be familiar.

I recommend only using this job search method for keeping track of a handful of your top companies and focusing more time and effort on some of the following job search methods.

Your Current Network

Another option for job searching is leveraging your current network of friends, family, and acquaintances. For this section, we're just talking about your existing network. I address the process of growing your network in Chapter 5, but for now, we'll just look at your current network.

Everyone already has a network that consists of people with whom you have some sort of connection. They might be people you know through a previous job, high school, college, hobby, or even distant family. Start by putting out "feelers" or letting people in your network know that you're looking for a new position. This doesn't mean you tell people in your network that they have to help you find a job. Instead, you're just informing your network that you are job searching and would appreciate any information they might have regarding positions available in your field of interest.

The plus side of leveraging your network is that the old adage "It's who you know" still rings true. Let's say you reach out to an old co-worker—we'll call him Carl—to tell him that you're searching for a new position. Carl says that his current employer has a position that would be a great fit for you. When you apply, you're able to mention in the cover letter that you learned about the job from Carl. A referral by a current employee makes you stand out from a crowd of job applicants. Not to mention that you wouldn't have even known about this position if Carl hadn't told you!

However, I should note that you really want to mainly leverage those in your network who can give a positive review of your experience and skills. If you have someone in your network who doesn't seem to like you very much, then you might want to avoid trying to leverage your connection with them as their opinion of you could negatively affect your chances for the job. Similarly, if you're associated with someone who is known as a lackluster employee at the company, your chances of being selected for a position could be drastically reduced, as the employer might assume you would be the same kind of poor worker as your connection.

Take stock of your existing network by making a list of all the people you know who might be able to recommend you for a job. Brainstorm people in your network who could be a stepping stone to connecting with someone else in your field. Jump to Chapter 5 for suggestions on how to build your network and instructions on how to reach out to these contacts.

Recruiters

Recruiters from recruiting agencies get a bad rap for some of the few bad apples that exist in the industry. As long as you understand the way recruiting works, then connecting with recruiters who represent positions in your field is a fantastic way for you to land a great job (and even get help negotiating a great salary!)

First, let's look at how recruiting works. Though a recruiter might be really nice to you and seem like your best friend, they are not working for you. That is, you are not their client. Instead, their client is the employer or company whose positions they are trying to fill. The good news about this setup is that most recruiters are being paid by the employer— not by you—to fill a position. There are some exceptions, but it's fairly rare for a recruiting agency to charge the job seeker a fee to connect them to a position.

The thing about recruiters or placement firms that you want to keep in mind is that some of them offer contract positions in which, though you'd work at a specific company, you'd actually be employed by the placement firm. In this situation, you would receive a paycheck directly from the placement firm rather than from the company at which you work. Though this can be a great way to get your foot in the door, many times it also means getting paid less or forgoing the health care and retirement benefits that you would have received as a direct employee of that company.

The plus side of working with a recruiter or placement firm is that some companies don't bother to post their open positions publicly. This means that unless you work with recruiters or placement firms, it's unlikely you would even know when a position with a certain company was available. Another potential bonus of working with recruiters is that some of them will actually negotiate your salary for you (and it's in the recruiter's best interest to get you the highest salary possible since most employers calculate the recruiter's fee based on your starting salary.)

The downside is that some placement firms require you to sign an exclusivity clause, which means you're not allowed to use any recruiters or placement firms other than them. If you decide to work with recruiters or placement firms, make sure to ask questions about how their services work.

Below is a list of recruiting organizations that have been successful in assisting some of my previous clients to connect with positions. However, you might want to consider looking for recruiting firms that specialize in your field or industry in order to more quickly and efficiently connect to job opportunities in your field.

- **Randstad** – Frequently has positions in many fields and at all levels within the manufacturing and production industry.
  *Veteran Friendly; www.Randstad.com
- **People Scout** – Represent positions across almost all industries.
  *Veteran Friendly; www.PeopleScout.com

- **AeroTek** – Originally represented positions in aerospace and defense; now represent a multitude of industries at all levels.
  *Veteran Friendly; www.AeroTek.com
- **RobertHalf** – Primarily has professional office-related roles at all levels.
  www.roberthalf.com

Job boards & Job Search Websites

Job boards are a specific location where employers go to post their open positions. With the rise of the internet, job boards are no longer relegated to a physical pegboard and can now be found online. This means that they can be updated quickly by employers when a job is filled or when a new position is open for applications.

Job boards can be very general and have positions across all industries posted on them, or they can be specialized and only cater to positions in specific fields. For example, dice.com (which is also a job search website) is specifically for positions related to information technology, while theatrejobboard.setc.org focuses specifically on theater-related positions. Run a quick search for your industry paired with the term "job board" in order to see if there are any job boards for your specific industry.

Job boards can also be used by multiple organizations to post positions located in a specific geographic area. One such geographically aligned job board to utilize would be your local Career One Stop's job board. Visit the national Career One Stop website (https://www.careeronestop.org/Site/american-job-center.aspx) where you can look up your local American Job Center. On the website for your local American Job Center, see if there is a list of open positions (the job board) for your region.

You can also consider looking at job boards that are created to help specific population demographics find positions. One example would be a job board created just for veterans like Recruitmilitary.com or a site like DisabilitySolutions.org, which is dedicated to assisting persons with disabilities connect with employment opportunities.

Probably one of the most utilized methods for finding open positions is through the use of national job search websites. Unlike job boards, a job search website actually allows you to run a search using specific keywords and scours multiple sources such as company websites and job boards. Some job search websites double as both a job board and a job search website. For example, Indeed.com allows employers to post specific positions on the site for a fee. However, when you use the site to search for a job, you'll get more job opportunities in your search results than just the ones that employers paid for. That's because the Indeed website scans other job boards and employer websites in order to provide you with more results for your job search.

A short list of national job search websites/job boards currently include:
- Ziprecruiter.com
- Indeed.com
- Monster.com
- Careerbuilder.com
- US.jobs

<u>**Next-Level Applications**</u>: **Apply through the company website**

While job search websites are great for helping you find open positions, they are not great for actually applying. Unfortunately, applying through a job search website merely adds another barrier between your application and the hiring manager. Even though an employer may post a position to a particular job search site, they might miss notifications from the job search site about recent applicants or worse, not be responsive to notifications at all.

Whenever possible, try to avoid applying through a third party (like a job search site) and instead see if you can apply for the job directly on the employer's website. Many job search sites will provide a link back to the employer's career webpage as part of the job post. However, there are times when no such link is provided. If a link to the employer's website isn't included in the job description, make a note of the job title and then run an online search using the name of that company and the job title. At the very least, this will generate a link for the company's career webpage. You can then peruse the company's posted job openings to find that particular position.

You may occasionally come across companies that don't have a career webpage. In this case, you may have to resort to applying directly through the job search website where you found the position listed. You may also find a position listed on a job search website, and, though the company has a career website, the position you hope to apply for isn't listed on it. This usually means that the position closed or has already been filled, but just hasn't been removed from the job search site. In these instances, if you're really interested in the position, you can look for a "Contact Us" page on the company's website and email them to inquire about the position.

How to Effectively Job Search

You would think that job searching would be easy what with all the job search website options; however, this is typically where most people get burnt out in the job search process. The reason this happens is that these folks have jumped into the job search without any kind of plan and with no knowledge of what keywords they should use for their job search.

Planning Ain't for Suckers

The biggest complaint about the job search I hear is that job seekers feel like they are applying for tons of positions and getting zero results. Essentially, they feel like they are "spinning their wheels" by putting in a ton of effort to spend hours scanning job search sites each day, then apply for five or six jobs in one sitting yet end up not getting any response from employers. If you do the math, these job seekers are applying for around 25-30 positions a week—yet they aren't getting any kind of bites on their applications. It's no wonder that these job seekers started to feel like applying for positions wasn't worth the effort!

Rather than spinning your wheels, I want to show you a method for creating a job search plan and the steps for getting job search results for positions that you're interested in applying for.

Suggestion 1: Limit how many job search websites you're using

Instead of visiting five to 10 job search websites, pick the top two to three sites that you've noticed have the most positions in your field. If you're worried about missing out on opportunities from those other sites you're dropping, set up an automatic job search on those sites so that you'll receive a weekly email with positions that match your job search parameters.

Suggestion 2: Set a goal for how many positions you're going to apply for each week

Submitting between three to five applications a week is more realistic than applying for 30 positions in a week. Lowering the number of positions you apply for will also provide you with more time to spend on each application. It's better to spend two days carefully updating your resume and completing an online application for one job than to sloppily apply for five jobs. You're more likely to get a call back from the one job that you took the time to tailor your application for.

Suggestion 3: Limit how often you job search each week

Setting an amount of time to spend on your job search each day helps you maintain your sanity during the job search process. Spending one to two hours a day searching and applying for jobs is just as effective (if not more effective!) than spending eight hours a day on the job search and application process.

Get Targeted in Your Approach

The above suggestions might seem counterintuitive to a successful job search. You would think that you'd land more interviews by applying for a ton of jobs, but unfortunately that method relies on a lot of luck. Basically, by applying for 30 jobs a week, you're taking a handful of darts and chucking them at a dartboard all at the same time in hopes that some will stick. And hey, maybe one will and you'll get an interview. But by using this method, the majority of your darts (or applications) are not going to stick and you'll have spent all that time applying for nothing.

Instead, if you start being more targeted and focusing on applying for one position at a time (throwing one dart), then you're more likely to get an interview (getting that dart to stick). Change your approach to the job search by carefully examining each position to determine if you meet all of the qualifications. Next, take the time to tailor your resume (as explained in Chapter 2) and build a cover letter (as detailed in Chapter 3). Take as long as you need to fully complete the application. Once you've applied for that one job, take a break and do something else to take your mind off the job search. You don't want to roll right into the next job application because your brain needs a break. If you try to complete too many job applications in one sitting, you'll start getting sloppy in your applications and will be less likely to get an interview for one of those jobs.

<u>**Next-Level Job Search**</u>: **Diversify your job search process**

I've worked with a lot of clients who prefer to stick to one job search method because it worked for them in the past. If it ain't broke, right? But if we're cutting the bullshit here, then I need to point out that using a specific job search method might work to land a role at a certain level of employment, but might not be effective in connecting to a position that is one or two levels higher on the career ladder. This is why it's so important to experiment with different methods of job searching. Continuing to only use a method that's worked for you in the past is likely to result in you only finding open roles that are still at your current level of employment. By mixing up your job search method, you're more likely to get different search results with positions at a variety of levels.

Identifying Useful Keywords

In order to more effectively search for positions for which you're a good fit, you need to identify keywords for your particular job search. Keywords are words or phrases used to find specific information when running a search. For job search purposes, keywords are going to be terms or phrases related to the type of job you're searching for. These could be potential job titles, the type of industry/field you're looking for employment in, or specific duties or responsibilities you want to have on a job. You'll start your search with a few keywords that are intuitive, and then as you job search, you'll discover more keywords and phrases that fit the type of position you're looking for.

Before you read any further, decide how you want to maintain a list of your keywords. The easiest method is to keep a pad of paper next to your computer and write down the keywords as you use them. Alternatively, you can maintain a spreadsheet or a Word document.

General Job Search Keywords

If you're seeking employment related to your experience or education but don't have a particular industry or job in mind, then it might feel tricky to come up with keywords. For a general job search like this, use keywords from your own experience and education to run a job search. For example, if you have a degree and want a job that requires a degree (which therefore might have a higher salary) use your specific degree to search. Using a job search website like Indeed.com, you can type in "Bachelor in Psychology," "Bachelor in Business Administration," or whatever your degree happens to be.

You could also search using specific duties you've had and plug in something like "data analysis" or "logistics." Another option would be to type in specific duties or responsibilities that you want to perform in a job such as "program development" or "social media outreach."

After each search, make a note on your notepad (or Word document) of the keyword or phrase you used in that search. If the keyword generated positions that look like a good fit, put a star next to that keyword on your notepad. If the keyword was a bust and you didn't get any interesting positions from it, mark that keyword out. This will keep you from wasting valuable time by retrying that useless keyword again in the future.

Specific Job Search Keywords

If you're focused on applying for positions in a specific field or industry, then you'll want to use keywords that are specific to that industry. Start by using keywords that might be a part of the job title. If you're looking for a position as a Theatre Director, then start by using that as your first keyword phrase on a job search site. If you're looking for a position as a Logistics Manager, then use that as your first keyword phrase.

Next, scroll through the jobs that pop up in your search and look at the job descriptions. If you feel like you match up to the position, then write down the job title of that position on your notepad and use that job title as a keyword phrase for your next search. By using the job title as a new keyword, you'll generate new positions that hadn't previously popped up in your search results. Doing this will also keep you from getting stuck in the rut of running the same job search over and over and getting the same results.

Am I Qualified?

A large part of the targeted job search process is determining whether or not you're qualified enough for a position to bother applying for it. Remember, you're not just hitting the apply button on tons of jobs anymore! Instead you're using a targeted approach and applying only for positions for which you're a good fit. If you're going to take the time to do this, then you want to make sure that you have the qualifications that the employer is looking for.

To determine if you're a good fit for a position, first scan the job description and look for a section labeled "Qualifications" or "Requirements." These are the skills, duties, education, and/or experience that an employer is telling you are required in order to be considered for this job. Sometimes there is wiggle room if you don't meet all the requirements. For example, if an employer is asking for 10 years of specific experience and you only have eight or nine years, then you can still apply. The same is true if the job description requires a degree and you're just about to graduate. In those instances, if you have all the other required qualifications, then an employer might overlook the fact that you don't meet one of the requirements.

However, if you find that you don't possess the skills listed or don't have the majority of the requirements listed in the job description, then you're very unlikely to be considered for an interview. Unless the job is with a company you've always dreamed of working for or you know someone at the company and they told you to apply anyway, then a job that you're not qualified for will not be worth applying to.

One of the best methods for determining if you should apply for a position is the highlighting method.

1) Print out the job description (or copy and paste it into a Word document).
2) Take a highlighter and scan the document looking for any duties, responsibilities, experience, skills, or education listed that you have. As you find a qualification that you have, highlight it.
3) Once finished, look at the overall document and all the highlighted sections. If it looks like 75% or more of the qualifications are highlighted: great! You should definitely apply for the job! But if you've only highlighted around 50% of the job description (or less), then it doesn't sound like you're a good fit for the role and it might not be worth it to take the time to apply for the position.

Next-Level Job Search: Saving job descriptions

Save the job descriptions for the positions to which you plan to apply. These will be useful for writing your resume, creating a cover letter, and preparing for an interview. There's nothing worse than being called for an interview and no longer being able to access the job description to use in preparation.

Chapter 2

Creating or Updating a Resume

If you've jumped to this chapter, then you either don't have a resume or the resume you're using hasn't been getting you enough (or any) interviews. This chapter can also be helpful if you haven't updated your resume for several years and want to make sure the information matches more modern resumes.

For those of you who are already getting interviews for the majority of the positions you apply for, I recommend you skip this section. There is no such thing as the "perfect resume," so don't waste time trying to achieve perfection. Instead, focus on effectively job searching, applying for positions, and improving your interview skills.

For those of you ready to update or create a resume, I cannot stress enough the importance of having a tailored resume. Though you'll mostly be filling out online applications and repeating some of the information within your resume, you will usually have an opportunity to upload a resume and cover letter. To be more marketable and present yourself as a professional, you'll need to upload a resume.

But what exactly do you include in a resume? To answer that, let's first look at what a resume should do for you.

The Purpose of a Resume

The only purpose of a resume is to get you the interview. That's it. The resume does not get you the job. I have never seen an employer look at a candidate's resume (with the exception of some direct-hire federal programs) and say, "That's the guy! Send him an offer letter right away!"

If only it were that simple. Instead, the resume is used by the employer to help determine if you're qualified for the job. They want to make sure that you have all of the required experience and education needed to be able to perform the role for which you applied. If you have all of those qualifications, then they may consider bringing you in for an interview. And then the interview is what gets you the job.

So why does creating a resume have to be so complicated if all it does is get you the interview? Unfortunately, a resume is no longer just a piece of paper with your previous employment experience and a few fancy terms like "professional," "top performer," "team player," or "leader." Though you might once have used a single version of your resume to apply for multiple positions without making any changes, those days of passing out your resume like a deck of cards are over. Instead, with the rise of the Applicant Tracking System, the whole ballgame changed. Now, in order to get an interview, you need to create a resume that provides a snapshot of your experience, education, skills, abilities, and accomplishments relevant to a particular job.

The following statement may sound harsh, but we're cutting the bullshit here, right?

Your resume is not about you—it's about what the hiring manager wants to know about you.

Though it can be difficult to separate your emotions from your professional experience and accomplishments, if you want to be successful in landing a position, then you need to be honest with yourself about which skills, experience, or accomplishments are important to a hiring manager… and which aren't. Hiring managers don't want to hear about skills and experience that aren't relevant to the position you applied for. Their job is to go through a stack of resumes and determine whether or not anyone in that pile has the experience, skills, and education required to be successful in a particular job.

Instead of including something on your resume because you think it's a "neat" or "cool" accomplishment, take a moment to consider if that accomplishment will actually seem relevant to the role for which you're applying. For example, you may be really proud that you ran a marathon, but it doesn't belong on your resume unless you're specifically applying to positions that have to do with running, marathons, or athletic activities. Sure, it will make you stand out to list it on your resume for a position unrelated to athletics, but only because of how inappropriate it is on your resume.

However, let's say you're applying for training and development roles and that you didn't just run the marathon, but also led a weekly running group during which you created personalized training plans and goals for the members. In that case, the details about how you trained other runners would be listed in a Volunteer Experience section with a breakdown of what you did in regards to training and development. Remember: always try to relate your experience back to the position you're applying for.

Applicant Tracking Systems

An Applicant Tracking System or ATS is a software system that helps manage the recruiting and hiring process. There are many different types of ATS out there, but the main thing you need to know is that an ATS is used to scan your resume and application for particular keywords that an employer has said are important to a job.

Here's the thing: ***Employers tell you in the job description what keywords they are looking for!*** You'll find keywords listed as required experience, skills, abilities, or specific education. If you can include the keywords from the job description in your resume, then the ATS system will note that your resume includes a high rate of the desired keywords. This means your resume is likely to be seen by a hiring manager, and you are then more likely to be selected for an interview. I'll get more detailed about keywords later and will give you step-by-step instructions for how to identify what keywords you should use in your resume depending on the industry.

Resume Length

There are only a few definite rules for resume writing, and document length is one of them. A professional resume should only be one to two pages long. That's it. Unless otherwise stated in the job description, do not go over two pages for your resume regardless of how much experience you have.

The free, downloadable resume template from my website (which you can find here: https://www.evergrowthcoach.com/resources) is two pages long, but if you have less experience or education, it's perfectly okay to only have a one-page resume. If you're using the resume for a job fair, you should consider shortening your resume to a single page since recruiters have less time at a job fair to review a two-page resume.

The only time you should use a longer resume is if you're applying for a federal position using a federal resume. The rest of the time, your resume should only be two pages. This is because employers simply don't have time to read more than two pages for each candidate. Even if you're at the executive level of your field and have over 30 years of experience in your industry, your resume is still expected to consist of two pages. Employers expect you to pare down the experience on your resume to only include information that is relevant to the position to which you're applying.

It is also recommended that you only list experience from the past 10 years. While this is not a definite resume rule, it is expected by most hiring managers that you won't go too much further than 10 years into your past experience. Positions held before that 10-year mark are usually considered to consist of outdated experience. (After all, just think about how drastically technology has changed the way we do things in the last 10 years across all industries.) However, if you have experience from 15 years ago that is your main argument for why you're qualified for the job to which you're applying, then you can go back 15 years in order to list that role.

Another exception to limiting your listed experience to the past 10 years is if you held positions for more than five or six years each. After all, if you only go back 10 years and you kept each position for five or more years, then you might end up only listing one to two positions on your resume! In this kind of scenario, you'll want to show that you have held other positions, especially if those roles are relevant to the position to which you're applying.

Sections No Longer Included in a Resume

There are going to be a few notably absent sections that you might have previously listed on your resume. These are the Objective and References sections. Listing these sections on the resume is an outdated practice and simply wastes space you could be using to market yourself to the employer.

Previously, an Objective was a statement of your purpose for applying to a position. If you couldn't include a cover letter and you just dropped off your physical resume with an employer, then the Objective section might have been useful to let the hiring manger know what job you were interested in. However, in today's job application process, you'll typically only be applying for one position at time through an online application, which automatically notes that you're applying for a specific role, so there's no need to mention the specific role in your resume.

The removal of the References section from your resume is for a similar reason. The online application process usually allows you to list your references and their contact information. Don't bother including the whole "References available upon request" line in the resume either. It is simply assumed by the employer that you'll provide a list of references when they ask.

That said, it is a good idea to create a separate document that lists your professional references and their contact information. For more information on references and suggestions on who you should include, jump to Chapter 5, which details preparing for the application process. To download a free references template, visit my website at https://www.evergrowthcoach.com/resources.

Identifying Industry-Specific Keywords

Before we update or build a resume, let's go ahead and create a list of keywords for your particular industry. Keywords will be words or phrases that are listed as requirements to be eligible for the applying to the position, or they will be skills mentioned over and over again in job descriptions for your industry. To identify keywords for your industry, follow these steps:

1) **Find job descriptions**
   Use an online job search site to find and review three to five job leads for your industry. (For a list of job search sites, revisit Chapter 1).

2) **Scan the job descriptions for keywords**
   You can manually read through each job description to look for words that are repeated across the different job postings. For example, if you're seeking employment in logistics, then you're likely to see the terms "logistics," "material handling," "inventory management," "warehouse," "shipping," or "distribution" scattered throughout the job descriptions. These would then be some of your industry-specific keywords.

   OR

You can use a free word cluster or word cloud generator to scan the job descriptions and identify the keywords for you. To do this, copy and paste the job descriptions into one blank computer document. Try not to copy general job posting information like Equal Employment Opportunity laws since that will throw off the process. The goal here is to end up with one really long word document. You'll then take that word document and copy and paste it into an online word cloud generator. Once you generate your word cloud, you'll see a grouping of words where some of the terms are larger in size than others. The words that are the largest in size are actually your industry keywords. Here are some great (free!) word cloud generators to check out that don't require a download.

- www.tagcloud.com
- www.wordclouds.com
- https://worditout.com/word-cloud/create

3) **Make a list of the top keywords for your industry/field**
   If you performed a manual search: Compile a list of the keywords you noticed when reviewing the job descriptions. If you used a word cloud generator: review the word cloud you generated and compile a list of the words that appeared in the largest size font.

   1. Determine if those keywords match your experience.
   2. Review that list of industry-specific keywords you just created. For each position you've held, determine if those keywords apply to the tasks you performed at that role or the skills you demonstrated while performing that job.

Now that you've developed a list of industry-specific keywords, we can move on to creating or updating your resume! Keep that list of keywords handy as we'll be using it soon to make the resume-building process much easier.

Creating a Resume from Scratch

If you already have a resume, skip this step and go to the Major Sections of a Resume. If you don't have a resume yet, it's smart to start by inputting your basic employment information into a resume template. I've posted a resume template on my website that you can download for free here: https://www.evergrowthcoach.com/resources. I've included both a Microsoft Word (for Windows users) and Pages version (for Mac users) so you can type directly into the template. Don't have either of those programs? Visit your local library or an American Job Center to use their onsite computers for free.

We're going to jump straight into the Professional Experience section of the resume and have you fill in general information about your employment history. Follow the next three steps to get started.

1) **Download a free resume template**
   Visit my website for a free resume template (https://www.evergrowthcoach.com/resources) or you can use a free template from Microsoft Word or Pages. You can also find a myriad of free resume templates online by doing a quick "free resume template" search. Just be wary of downloading anything from a website that doesn't look trustworthy. I also recommend avoiding resume templates that use colors or pictures.

2) **Fill in your previous positions**
   Skip the Summary of Qualifications and Key Skills sections as they can be overwhelming. Don't worry, we'll get to them later. For now, you're going to focus only on the Professional Experience section. Starting with your most recent or current position, fill out the information for your employment history including job title, company name, city, and state. Include the month/year you started and the month/year you left the position. I also recommend only listing the positions you've had in the last 10 years. However, if you need to go back a little further to capture a position that's important for the roles you'll be applying for, then that's completely okay.

3) **Add your industry keywords**
   For each position listed, review the industry keywords you identified earlier. If a keyword in your list applies to your experience during a specific role, you can type the keyword in under that position next to the bullets. Remember, we're keeping it simple for now, so don't worry about trying to make anything sound fancy. Later, you're going to use these keywords to help you create detailed experience bullets that are relevant to the positions to which you're applying. You may find that you're listing a lot of keywords for each position and that's completely okay! More keywords now will actually make it easier to build out detailed sentences later.

Major Sections of a Resume

Contact Information

Now that you've identified some keywords for your particular industry, let's jump into the resume starting with your Contact Information at the very top. From there, I'll walk you through each section of your resume and will explain how to fill each section with the information that is the most likely to capture a hiring manager's attention (in a good way of course).

All of your contact information will appear at the top of your resume. If you're using the resume template I've provided, you'll see there is a section at the top where you can type in your first name, middle initial (optional), and last name. You'll also fill in your physical address, phone number, and email address in this section.

If you are applying to positions in another city, you may want to consider not listing your physical address. There are some employers who will not bother to look at a resume if the applicant is from another city or state.

It has also become a fairly common practice to only list one's city and state on the resume instead of the full address. This can keep employers from judging your socioeconomic status based on your zip code.

For those using their own resume formatting, do not list your contact information in the header section. Instead, your contact information should be a part of the document's body, not inserted as a header. The reason to avoid listing your contact information in the header section is that when you upload your resume to an employer's online portal, they may not be able to view the header section—which means they won't have your contact information to call you for an interview.

<u>Next-Level Contact Information</u>: LinkedIn profile address

If you've already created a professional LinkedIn profile, you can add the URL/website address for your LinkedIn profile in the Contact Information section of your resume after your email address. I tend to include the address for my LinkedIn profile, but I remove the hyperlink to both my LinkedIn profile address and my email address. Removing the hyperlinks will keep your email and LinkedIn profile link from affecting how the resume is processed by an online application system.

I also recommend removing any hyperlinks if you're emailing your resume as an attachment to an employer. When some email servers detect a hyperlink in an attached document, they automatically send that email to a spam or junk folder. Don't let this happen to you!

To remove a hyperlink from a web address or email address on your resume in Microsoft Word, right click on the address, then look for the option: "Remove Hyperlink." You'll still have the information listed for the LinkedIn profile address or email address, but it will no longer be a blue hyperlink.

Summary of Qualifications

SUMMARY OF QUALIFICATIONS

U.S. Army Veteran with a Bachelor's in Global Supply Chain Management and over 15 years of experience planning, coordinating, and managing logistical operations in local, national, and global environments. Proven track record in analyzing material handling procedures to identify areas of improvement and successfully developed a distribution process which increased productivity by 15% while decreasing costs. Experienced in training and supervising personnel, assigning projects, providing performance evaluations, and fostering an environment of professional growth. Regularly manage the receipt, storage, inventory, maintenance, and distribution of over $5 million worth of equipment and materials.

Arguably one of the most important sections of your resume (no pressure!), the Summary of Qualifications is a paragraph that sums up your experience, education, and skills relevant to the job. This section will typically consist of five to six sentences that provide a hiring manager with a brief snapshot of why you're a great fit for the role to which you're applying. A good Summary of Qualifications section will entice a hiring manager into wanting to learning more about your experience so that they'll actually read the rest of your resume.

The information within those five to six sentences should be tailored toward the specific position for which you're applying. The great thing is that you don't have to guess what the employer wants to know about you because they told you that in the job description! If you followed the previous steps for identifying industry-specific keywords, then you have a good start on the information most employers in your industry will be looking for. Before applying for a role, you'll take keyword identification one step further by specifically reading through the job description and identifying the skills, experience, and education listed as required for that specific position.

The Summary of Qualifications can feel like a really difficult and overwhelming section to write. Whenever I create a resume for clients, I always save this section for last. After all, it is a "summary" of your resume. How can you create a summary of something you haven't finished writing yet? Rather than jumping into the Summary of Qualifications right now, I recommend that you complete the rest of the resume first, then come back to this section later. It will make it a heck of a lot easier to write.

Ready to Create a Summary of Qualifications

You've finished all the other sections of your resume and you're ready to create a strong Summary of Qualifications that will capture the hiring manager's attention. The first thing you want to do is review the job description. Take note of specific experience, education, or abilities that the employer has listed as being required for the job. Those are the main items you'll want to list in your Summary to show that you're a strong applicant. Try to stay away from using too many "filler words" as they only take up space and will not help you get through the Applicant Tracking System. Filler words are usually things like "successful," "high achiever," or "top performer." I've also heard these terms referred to as "power words" and, while they can be helpful in making a powerful statement (when used sparingly), they also take up space for keywords that an employer's ATS is actually scouring your resume for. Instead of taking up valuable space in your Summary with these filler words, focus on incorporating the keywords from the job description. Then, if you have space left and need more oomph for your Summary of Qualifications, you might add a few power words to the mix.

The first sentence of the Summary is going to be the most important since it's the first thing the hiring manager will typically read. You want to pack it with information about your experience relevant to the job without making it too lengthy. A good rule of thumb is that the opening sentence should not be more than two lines long.

Here are a few Summary of Qualifications examples to help you craft your own Summary. Feel free to use the same language from the examples below in your Summary!

Example 1:

U.S. Army Veteran with a Bachelor's in Global Supply Chain Management and over 15 years of experience planning, coordinating, and managing logistical operations in local, national, and global environments. Proven track record in analyzing material handling procedures to identify areas of improvement and successfully developed a distribution process which increased productivity by 15% while decreasing costs. Experienced in training and supervising personnel, assigning projects, providing performance evaluations, and fostering an environment of professional growth. Regularly manage the receipt, storage, inventory, maintenance, and distribution of over $5 million worth of equipment and materials.

Example 2:

Current Information Systems and Cybersecurity student with experience analyzing, updating, and maintaining information security systems. Proven track record in identifying information assurance risks and conducting penetration tests to determine system vulnerabilities. Regularly troubleshoot, diagnose, and resolve hardware, software, network, and security system issues while providing a quality customer service experience for internal and external end-users. Possess the Security+, Network+, and A+ CompTIA certifications with an ability to communicate technical concepts across all levels of an organization.

Example 3:

Health Services Manager with a Master's in Healthcare Administration and over 17 years of experience in administrative management across various healthcare environments. Proven track record in program development and improvement through data analysis and optimization of productivity. Experienced in managing teams of personnel, delegating assignments, providing performance evaluations, and fostering an environment of professional growth. Regularly managed data, information, and sensitive records using various software applications and databases. Able to communicate across all levels of an organization and with external agencies or vendors to build strategic partnerships. Possess the Project Management Professional (PMP) Certification.

Example 4:

Innovative marketing manager with a Bachelor's in Business Administration and extensive experience communicating program and product information to potential customers. Proven track record in conducting high-impact outreach and marketing campaigns, coordinating events, and completing follow-ups to retain customers. Regularly create, organize, and maintain documentation, managing information databases to input data, generate reports, and analyze trends in data to develop future marketing strategies. Experienced in developing strategic partnerships with external agencies or organizations to meet marketing objectives.

Example 5:

Licensed Counseling Intern with a Master's in Marriage and Family Therapy and experience in individual counseling, group facilitation, and case management. Proven track record in maintaining clinical case records and documentation in accordance with HIPAA regulations and organizational policies. Experienced in conducting client intake and administering mental status assessments before developing a differential diagnosis and creating Individual Treatment Plans (ITPs) with patient input. Experienced in building relationships with local community organizations, nonprofits, and state or federal agencies to develop referral options for clients.

Whenever you apply to a new position, you'll always want to go back and tweak this Summary of Qualifications section to more accurately reflect your experience as related to the position's requirements. Try to keep your Summary short and to the point. If the Summary starts to get too lengthy, hiring managers might not bother to read it. When adding new information to your Summary, review the other information already there to determine if you can remove something that's less relevant to the job you're applying for in order to keep the Summary short and to the point.

Key Skills

```
┌─────────────────────────────────────────────────────────────────────────────┐
│                                 KEY SKILLS                                    │
│                                                                               │
│  Program & Project Management ♦ Strategic Planning ♦ Inventory & Resource     │
│  Management ♦ Logistics & Supply                                              │
│  Policy Development ♦ Process Improvement ♦ Supervision & Training ♦ Quality  │
│  Control ♦ Safety Compliance                                                  │
└─────────────────────────────────────────────────────────────────────────────┘
```

This is probably my favorite section of the resume. Including a Key Skills section helps you get more of those keywords from the job description into your resume, and it's an easy section to fill out and update in order to tailor your resume for each position to which you apply.

Go ahead and get out that list of industry-specific keywords. For now, type those keywords into the Key Skills section. Don't worry about being too lengthy right now. When you go to apply for a specific position, you'll cut your Key Skills section down to just 2 lines to ensure that hiring managers will be more likely to read it.

While typing these key skills in, notice how they're written. Remember that it's a list of your key skills, not a list of your titles. So instead of saying, "Project Manager," you'd say, "Project Management."

If the positions you're applying for don't have very good job descriptions, it might be difficult to come up with strong key skills to list in this section. Below are some general key skills that most employers would be happy to have in an employee. However, remember that these are generic skills and are not tailored toward a specific field. If possible, it's always better to list skills that are relevant to the position for which you're applying.

A Short List of Key Skills

Time Management	Conflict Resolution	Safety Compliance
Communication	Customer Service	Problem-Solving
Personnel Supervision	Performance Evaluations	Training & Instruction
Documentation & Reports	Database Management	Relationship Development
Sales	Administration	Program Management
Presentations & Briefs	Planning	Quality Control

A big note for this section is to never use an automated table. (I know, I know—I used an automated table above to give you a list of key skill examples, but that was just for informational purposes, not for formatting your resume.) While an automated table would allow you to potentially list a lot more skills, most online application systems do not process information listed in tables very well. Instead, separate your skills with a neutral symbol like a diamond or a vertical line. Most word processing systems have an option to insert symbols into a word document. Check out the resume templates provided at the back of this book to see Key Skills formatting that is acceptable to online application systems.

Your Key Skills section might look something like the following examples. Notice how with each example you can get a general feel for that applicant's experience just by scanning the Key Skills and can guess what type of positions they are applying for.

Example 1:

Key Skills

Marketing & Outreach ♦ Copywriting ♦ Social Media Campaigns ♦ Data Analysis
Project Management ♦ Strategic Partnership Development ♦ Public Relations

Example 2:

Key Skills

Accounts Payable ♦ Reports & Auditing ♦ Customer Service ♦ Records Management
Payroll Processing ♦ Quality Control ♦ Project Management ♦ Document Review

Example 3:

Key Skills

Emergency Management ♦ Supervision & Training ♦ Quality Assurance Inventory Control ♦
Environmental Health & Safety ♦ Project Management ♦ Policy Development

This is one of the easiest sections to tailor toward positions to which you're applying, so remember to update your Key Skills section each time you apply for a new position! Doing so will help you get through those Applicant Tracking Systems as you can use the Key Skills section to incorporate keywords from the job description into your resume.

Professional Experience

PROFESSIONAL EXPERIENCE

Job Title (most recent or current)   Month Year – Month Year
Company, City, State
- (Insert experience, duties, responsibilities, or accomplishments here)
-
-
-

Job Title   Month Year – Month Year
Company, City, State
- |
-
-
-

Job Title   Month Year – Month Year
Company, City, State
-
-
-
-

     Notice that I don't call this section Work History or Employment History. I like the headline for this section to be Professional Experience as I want to capture any experience that is considered relevant to the job. That might mean listing unpaid internships or fellowships. In some cases, you can even list volunteer experience.

     A good rule of thumb for this section is to only list your employment from the last 10 years or so. Of course, there are always exceptions depending on your particular situation. If you're applying for positions in an industry that you previously worked in more than 10 years ago, then you might want to list some of those old positions. This means you might have to compress or shorten some of your more recent positions in order to have room to list those older positions. If you're concerned about not showing enough work history, you could also list some of your older employment as demonstrated in the Example Resume 2, which can be found in the Resources section of this book.

     If you haven't already, go ahead and start filling in the professional experience section of your resume. You'll list your positions in reverse chronological order, which means you'll start with your most recent (or current) position first and will work backwards from there.

The majority of the basic information like your job title and company name is fairly self-explanatory. However, I do want to expand on one thing: job titles. When employers first review your resume, they scan it for an average of 7 seconds. During those 7 seconds, one of the main things they review are your job titles to see if any of those titles match up to the position for which you're applying. It's okay if you haven't held the exact same job title as the position to which you're applying, but there are some options to make it match up a little better.

One option is to list your official job title in the resume, then, in parentheses, list a title that better matches the position to which you're applying. An example would be if your official job title was very vague, like "Coordinator," then you might add a little explainer in parentheses to help employers understand what you did just from your job title.

Title Update Example 1:
Official Title: Coordinator
Updated Title: Coordinator (Events & Conferences)

Remember, you're trying to match up the job title for the position to which you're applying. As such, the above example would be great if you're applying to be an event coordinator, but not so great if you're applying to be a social coordinator. For that, you might instead say: Coordinator (Social Events).

Important Note: Never stretch the truth anywhere in your resume. If you list a skill or job title in your resume, then you must be able to back that information up in an interview if asked about it. I've seen applicants with information in their resume that stretched the truth a little too much—to the point where they were called out in the interview (and most certainly did not get the job). Always make sure you feel comfortable being able to provide an explanation for the experience or job titles you list in your resume.

Another issue with your titles which you might tackle using parentheses is incorporating your level of employment in your job title if it's not obvious. For example, if you were a manager at your last position, but your official title doesn't include the term manager, then you can add it in parentheses.

Title Update Example 2:
Official Title: Logistics Technician
Updated Title: Logistics Technician (Area Manager)

Experience Bullet Basics

Now it's time to focus on the meat of the resume: explaining your actual experience and responsibilities for each position. This may seem daunting, but don't worry! That's why we identified keywords for your industry earlier.

A question I get a lot is how many bullets should each position have? A good rule of thumb is to try to list 3-6 experience bullets per position. If you performed fewer responsibilities at a position or had less relevant duties in a role, then you might only list three bullets. For other positions, you may find that you have way too many experience bullets and have to cut them down. Unfortunately, hiring managers just don't have time to read all of your bullets anyway. If they see that you have more than seven bullets listed for a position or have more than seven bullets listed for every position, then they might not bother to continue reading your resume.

Try to pare down your experience bullets to include only the experience relevant to the position for which you're applying. Another option is to merge some of your bullets together to make one bullet (without making it too long).

Speaking of the length of the experience bullet, most employers prefer for experience bullets to only be one to two lines long. In order to be very clear in communicating your experience to employers, keep every bullet one simple sentence.

Lastly, it's up to you if you want to have a period at the end of your experience bullets or not. I prefer to include a period at the at the end of experience bullets, but it's not required. Some will even argue that you shouldn't have periods at the end of a bulleted sentence, but as long as you're being consistent throughout the Professional Experience section in either using a period or not using a period, then it really doesn't matter.

Creating Experience Bullets

Always try to start your sentences with a verb as it makes the information more interesting. If you're currently working in a role, then you'll use present tense verbs. If you're listing experience for a role you no longer have, then you'll use past tense verbs since you performed those duties and responsibilities in the past.

Present Job Examples:
- Receive, store, and inventory fragile materials and perishable goods, periodically inspecting items to identify expired items or remove damaged goods.
- Manage 12 customer service representatives, creating weekly schedules, monitoring hours worked, and submitting payroll information for each employee.

Previous/Past Job Examples:
- Answered a multi-line phone in a fast-paced call center environment and provided a quality customer service experience, which increased customer satisfaction and retention.
- Troubleshot, diagnosed, and resolved software, hardware, or networking issues while providing a positive customer service experience.
- Managed and coordinated daily activities to ensure the appropriate execution of human resource and personnel actions for over 750 staff members.

Starting each sentence with a strong verb helps keep the employer or hiring manager interested. Try to avoid starting sentences with things like, "Responsible for" or "Tasked with." It's not wrong to use these, but they are little more passive and don't make as much of an impact on an employer.

Strengthening Bullet Example 1:
<u>Weak</u>: Responsible for developing strategic partnerships with external organization.
<u>Strong</u>: Develop strategic partnerships and business relationships with external organizations.

Strengthening Bullet Example 2:
<u>Weak</u>: Tasked with assessing production processes and implementing more effective methods.
<u>Strong</u>: Assess production processes in order to identify and implement more effective methods.

By cutting the weaker words from the beginning, you'll also be able to fit more information into the sentence and expand it to be more detailed.

For a list of strong action verbs you can use to start your sentences, jump to the Action Verbs list included in the Resources section.

Crafting Detailed Experience Bullets

It's time to start writing your experience bullets (or updating the experience in your current resume). Hopefully you've already added information from that list of industry-specific keywords you created in this earlier section. If you skipped that section, I highly recommend that you go back and complete that step. Having a list of industry-specific keywords will give you a starting point for what to include in your experience bullets.

Once you've got that list of keywords, look through your previous positions and review your list of keywords. For each position, ask yourself if you performed any tasks that involved those industry-specific keywords. (For those of you who already completed this step in an earlier chapter, you can roll on to the next paragraph.)

Next, you're going to create a sentence based on one or more keywords from your list.

If your list of keywords looks something like this:
- Supervising
- Performance evaluation
- Professional development
- Budget management
- Project management
- Assigning tasks

Then, focusing on a few of those keywords, you might create sentences like this:

- Supervised personnel, assigning tasks and monitoring progress to ensure projects were completed within timeline.
- Managed a department budget, approving and monitoring expenditures for equipment or supplies required to meet organizational goals.
- Provided performance evaluations, identifying areas of individual improvement and suggesting professional development, which increased individual performance.

You'll notice that I combined some of the keywords to create the first sentence (supervising and assigning tasks) and did the same thing for the second sentence in order to include more keywords in one sentence (performance evaluation and professional development). However, the third sentence only included one keyword and expanded on that experience.

It may not be possible to use your industry-specific keywords for all of your positions. If you need more information for a position, ask yourself, "What were my main responsibilities?" and "What was my proudest accomplishment at that position?" These questions can help you come up with more examples of experience or responsibilities that you performed at those positions.

Next-Level Resume Writing: Quantifying Your Experience

While it's great to have detailed sentences explaining your relevant experience, duties, and responsibilities, employers will be more likely to be impressed if you can quantify your experience with specific numbers or percentages. Unfortunately, many job seekers feel intimidated about adding numbers to their resume and aren't sure where to start, or they don't think that their field or industry even has information that can be quantified.

First, to keep you from feeling intimidated, know that you don't have to add numbers to every bullet (and in fact, that would be overkill if you did). Second, applicants from any field or industry can find ways to quantify their experience or accomplishments.

The easiest method for inserting numerical values into your resume is to review your experience bullets and ask yourself, "How much?" or "How many?" for some of them. Some bullets are easier to quantify than others.

Looking at those last few bullet points of experience we added, let's see if we can quantify them.

Original Bullet Examples:

- Supervised personnel, assigning tasks and monitoring progress to ensure projects were completed within timeline.
- Managed a department budget, approving and monitoring expenditures for equipment or supplies required to meet organizational goals.
- Provided performance evaluations, identifying areas of individual improvement and suggesting professional development, which increased individual performance.

Let's focus on the first bullet. The main focus of that sentence is that you supervised personnel. Applying the "How much/How Many?" question, you would ask yourself, "How many personnel did I supervise?" If you supervised 10 personnel, then you could include that in the bullet.

Quantified Experience Bullet 1:
- Supervised 10 personnel, assigning tasks and monitoring progress to ensure projects were completed within timeline.

Looking at the next bullet, apply the "How much/How many?" question to see how we can add some kind of quantifiable information.

Original Bullet 2:
- Managed a department budget, approving and monitoring expenditures for equipment or supplies required to meet organizational goals.

Here, the main subject is that you managed a department budget, so the easiest question to ask is how much your budget was. This might lead to the following more quantified bullet:

Quantified Experience Bullet 2:
- Managed a department budget of over $200,000, approving and monitoring expenditures for equipment or supplies required to meet organizational goals.

Since you've added quantifiable information to two of the experience bullets for one job, you don't need to add numbers to the last experience bullet, but I want to show you how to quantify your experience with percentages, so let's go ahead and examine that last experience bullet.

Original Bullet 3:
- Provided performance evaluations, identifying areas of individual improvement and suggesting professional development, which increased individual performance.

This one is a little trickier. You could focus on how many performance evaluations you conducted and add that number, but chances are that if you supervised 10 personnel, that you probably performed 10 performance evaluations. You don't want to repeat a number you've already used. That's just a waste of space as it doesn't really add information to your resume that the hiring manager hasn't already read in another section of your resume.

Instead, let's focus on the last part of the sentence, "…suggesting professional development which increased individual performance." Ask yourself, "how much did my suggestions improve these individuals' work performance?" This might be difficult if your particular industry doesn't use metrics to track and record individual employee's performance. However, if you work in sales or marketing and your training suggestions resulted in an uptick in sales, then you could mention the percentage of increased sales. Or if you're in customer service and your training suggestions resulted in improved customer satisfaction, then you could note the percentage increase of customer satisfaction.

Quantified Bullet 3: (For Sales)
- Provided performance evaluations, identifying areas of individual improvement and suggesting professional development, which increased staff performance and resulted in a 25% sales increase.

Quantified Bullet 3: (For Customer Service)

- Provided performance evaluations, identifying areas of individual improvement and suggesting professional development, which resulted in increased customer service satisfaction by 30%.

If you're feeling stuck and aren't sure what kind of questions you should ask in order to add more quantifiers to your resume, here is a list of questions you might ask for each role:

- How many customers served?
- How many line-items of inventory?
- How much was the equipment worth that you were responsible for?
- How much money did you save your company with a new idea?
- How much in sales did you make for your company?
- By what percentage did you improve your company's production line?
- How many employees did you hire?
- How many employees did you train or help onboard?
- How much did the updates you made to an SOP improve safety/production/etc.?

For each position of employment listed, see if you can insert quantifiable information into at least two bullets. Even if you don't ultimately end up using those bullets in their quantified form, it's good to have those numbers in the back of your mind to use in interviews if needed.

A Note on Numbers: When adding numerical values to your resume, there is always the question of whether you should write out the number (one, four, seven, etc.) or leave it in its numerical form (1, 4, 7). The standard English rule is that numbers from 1-10 should be written out. However, in a resume, writing out a number can actually make it lose the impact a numerical number would have. As a result, I tend to prefer listing numbers in their numerical form with the exception of dollar amounts in the millions. You don't want to waste resume space with too many zeroes, so in those instances, you could write, "$5 million," instead of, "$5,000,000."

It's up to you how you list your numbers, but as long as you're consistent and don't switch back and forth between writing out numbers and listing them in their numerical form, then you'll be fine.

Education & Specialized Training

EDUCATION & SPECIALIZED TRAINING

- Bachelor of Science, Major, School, City, State, Month Year Graduation
- Name of License, Issuing Organization, Year Completed, License #: XXXX
- Name of Certificate or Training, Issuing Organization, Year Completed

---

The next section to tackle is listing your education, training, professional licenses, and/or relevant professional certifications. While it would be great if you could list all of your specialized training, employers would much rather you only list the education and specialized training relevant to the position for which you're applying. For those who have a lot of training and education to list, you'll need to determine what is the most important education or training to list for the job. If you have a long list of relevant training and education even after you've removed the irrelevant trainings, then you may need to include sub-headers in this section in order to break up the information to make it easier for employers to read.

The main listing in this section is usually any formal postsecondary education. There are no rules about the order in which you should list your education, but I tend to prefer listing your most recent degree (or the degree you're currently working on) first. If you're currently working on a degree or have finished a degree, then there's no need to list a high school diploma.

Listing More Than One Degree Education Example:
- Master of Business Administration (MBA), Focus: Data Analysis, Columbia University, New York, NY, May 2018
- Bachelor of Science, Business Administration, Minor: International Relations, Tennessee State University, Nashville, TN, December 2015

Currently Completing a Degree Education Example:
- (Currently) Bachelor of Science, Psychology, West Virginia University, Morgantown, WV, Expected Graduation: May 2021

Listing College Credit (Not Currently Enrolled) Education Example:
- 56 Semester Credit Hours, Bachelor of Arts, English, Minor: Creative Writing, University of Maine, Orono, ME

You'll notice that we don't list your GPA, honors, or specific courses. Most civilian employers aren't interested in that kind of information unless you don't have a lot of experience to show. However, if you're qualifying for the position solely based on your education, then it would be wise to include some of those items.

Using Education to Qualify for Job Education Example:
- Bachelor of Business Administration (BBA), Systems Information, University of North Dakota, Grand Forks, ND, May 2018, GPA: 3.8
  Relevant Coursework: Information Security; Introduction to Programming for Data Analytics; Fundamentals of Database Management; Fundamentals of Networking

Next, let's look at best methods for listing any current (or relevant but expired) licenses. These are professional licenses that are usually required to work in an industry. Again, make sure to only list licenses that are relevant to the position to which you're applying. It doesn't help your odds of landing an interview to list irrelevant licenses as they'll only distract a hiring manager from the more relevant information in your resume. So, if you still hold a license from being a real estate agent 10 years ago, but you're applying to be a logistics manager for a warehouse, then it's probably not going to be a relevant license to list. However, if you were applying to be a property manager, then that real estate license might help you gain an edge over the other applicants since it's relevant to the role.

Key information to include when listing a license is the name of the license, the issuing organization, state, or federal agency, the year issued, the license number, and, if applicable, the year the license expires.

Licenses Examples:
- Clinical Professional Counselor License, State of Maine, Issued: May 2015, License #: 5555
- Tennessee Private Investigator License, Private Investigation & Polygraph Commission, Issued: July 2015, License #: 5555
- Commercial Driver's License (CDL), State of Florida, Issued: May 2002, Expires: May 2020, License #: FL55555

Lastly, let's look at listing professional certifications. With these, you want to make sure you're listing the official name of the certification, the issuing organization, and the year it was issued or the year it expires.

Professional Certification Examples:
- Cardiopulmonary Resuscitation (CPR) & First Aid Certification, American Heart Association, Expires: May 2021
- Project Management Professional (PMP) Certification, Project Management Institute, June 2017
- Black Belt Certification, Lean Six Sigma, July 2018
- A+, CompTIA, Expires: June 2021
- Certified Occupational Safety Specialist (COSS), Occupational Health and Safety Administration (OSHA), January 2017
- Leadership Development (Supervisor) Course, U.S. Army, September 2016

Note: For military certifications or trainings, consider adding a one- or two-word explanation for the course in parentheses. Check out Resume 3 in the Resources section for an example.

Once you put your education, specialized training, and certifications together, it might look something like this:

Education & Specialized Training Example 1:
- Master of Social Work, University of Iowa, Iowa City, IA, May 2017

- Bachelor of Science, Social Work, California State University, Los Angeles, CA, May 2015
- Licensed Clinical Social Worker (LCSW), State of Iowa, Issued: May 2019, License #: IA5555
- Rapid Resolution Therapy Certification, Institute for Rapid Resolution Therapy, June 2019

As previously mentioned, if you have a lot of relevant training or a certification, you can add a sub-header. In that case, the education section might look something like this:

Education & Specialized Training Example 2:
- Bachelor of Science, Environmental Health and Safety, University of Houston, Houston, TX, May 2016
- Green Belt, Lean Six Sigma, June 2017
- Chemical, Biological, Explosive, Radiological, and Nuclear (CBRN) Specialist Course, U.S. Army, September 2010

FEMA Certifications:
- IS-27, Orientation to FEMA Logistics, May 2016
- IS-29.a, Public Information Officer Awareness, June 2016
- IS-3, Radiological Emergency Management, July 2016
- IS-100, Introduction to the Incident Command System, ICS-100, May 2016

Try to keep your list of education, training, and certifications to six bullet points or fewer, otherwise employers will stop reading since the list is too long. This means you may have to determine which trainings and certifications are the most important and only list those that make the cut. (Remember to always look back at the job description to get an idea of what the employer is looking for! They might even mention specific certifications or training requirements for the job, which will give you a better idea of what to list in this section.)

Optional Sections of a Resume

If you still have space on your resume and wish to include your relevant volunteer experience, awards, publications, or technical skills, feel free to do so! However, remember that the key word here is relevant.

Awards

Just because you earned an Employee of the Year Award 15 years ago, doesn't mean it should go on your resume. If you earned the award for performing a task that's relevant to the position for which you're applying, then it's worth listing. But if you're listing it simply to beef up your resume, then I bet that you have other experiences that would make better use of your resume space than an old award that you can't give a specific reason for having earned.

If you only have a short list of awards—let's say two to four to list in this section—then you may consider listing the awards with a very brief explanation for them.

Awards Section Example 1:
- Earned 2019 Employee of the Year at XYZ Inc. for exceeding sales quota by 25%
- Awarded Top Seller 2018 by the National Sales & Marketing Association

If you have a long list of awards, consider cutting them down to only include the top awards or the most recent awards. Just like with other lists, employers tend to stop reading if the list gets too lengthy.

Alternatively, with a short list like the above example, you could forgo having a separate awards section and instead mention your award in the Professional Experience section by listing it as the last experience bullet for the role at which you earned the award. Your position listing in the Professional Experience section might then look something like this:

Professional Experience with Award Included Example:
Area Manager   July 2013 – January 2017
XYX Inc., Dover, TN
- Supervised personnel, assigning tasks and monitoring progress to ensure projects were completed within timeline.
- Managed a department budget, approving and monitoring expenditures for equipment or supplies required to meet organizational goals.
- Earned 2019 Employee of the Year for exceeding sales quota by 25% and awarded Top Seller of 2018 by the National Sales & Marketing Association

Volunteer Experience

Similar to listing awards, a section of volunteer experience should only include experience that is relevant to the position to which you're applying. If you volunteer at an animal shelter and you're applying for a role at a veterinarian's office, then you should definitely include that volunteer experience! But if you're applying for a position as a data analyst, then that volunteer experience at the animal shelter is not as relevant (unless one of your tasks at the animal shelter was to research and analyze data).

If your volunteer position is the main experience that qualifies you for a position, then I would instead recommend listing that position under the Professional Experience section. If you decide to go with this option, make sure to mention that it's a volunteer role and not a paid position. It might look something like this:

Volunteer Role as Professional Experience Example:
Greeter & Customer Coordinator (Volunteer)   May 2016 – May 2017

- Putnam County Animal Shelter, Putnam County, NY
- Greeted visitors, explaining shelter adoption regulations and answering visitor questions.
- Maintained a clean and organized front office environment, restocking supplies as needed and performing general cleaning tasks.
- Introduced animals to visitors while ensuring the safety of both the animals and guests.

I also urge caution on mentioning volunteer experience earned from religious institutions or those that are politically affiliated. If you're applying to roles with organizations which hold those same beliefs or political ideology, then it's okay to list that volunteer experience. However, when applying for roles with organizations that do not have any specific religious leanings or political affiliations, consider leaving off that volunteer experience unless you performed duties at that volunteer position that make you a great candidate for the role.

This is not an attempt to stifle your personal, religious, or political beliefs. Instead, leaving that information out of your resume may keep you from experiencing discrimination. You may not even know that you're being discriminated against since an employer or hiring manager who is turned off by that kind of information on your resume will simply not call you for an interview. Try to avoid this situation by not mentioning anything political or religious on your resume if possible.

Publications

Similar to awards, including a list of publications on a resume is optional and should only be used if the publications are relevant to a position to which you're applying. For example, though I've written several books, I wouldn't include my works of fiction on my resume if I applied for a position in the career services industry. While I'm proud to have written those books, they aren't relevant to career services and as such, shouldn't be included in my resume.

Publications Example:
- "Motivating the Unmotivated," Professional Development Book, Random House, 2017.
- Doe, J. (2016, Fall). "Managing Professional Development with Remote Employees." Journal of American Professional Development.

Organizational Affiliations & Professional Memberships

This is different from the Volunteer Experience section as this section will usually just involve a list of organizations, your membership status, and the timeframe of your membership/affiliation. A tight Organizational Affiliations section might look something like this:

Organizational Affiliation Example:
- Vice-President, American Counseling Association, 2018 – Present; Member, 2015 – Present
- Member, National Association of Counseling Professionals, 2016 – Present
- Member, Veteran Mental Health & Wellness Initiative Program, 2016 – Present

Like everything else in your resume, make sure to only list the organization affiliations or memberships that are relevant to the position to which you're applying.

Technical Skills

When applying for positions in information technology or roles that require experience with specific types of software or hardware, I recommend including a Technical Skills section. When listing the software, hardware, or other technical skills you have, make sure that these are things you would feel comfortable doing on a job. Don't list computer programs or hardware that you've heard of but have never used.

If you're applying for a position that mentions a specific software, you might have a Technical Skills section that looks like this:

TECHNICAL SKILLS

Adobe Illustrator ♦ Adobe Dreamweaver ♦ Salesforce ♦ Tableau ♦ Final Cut Pro

And if you're in an information technology field, then you might replace the Key Skills section with a Technical Skills section that looks like this:

TECHNICAL SKILLS

Operating Systems: Windows XP, Windows Vista, Windows 7/8/10, Microsoft Virtual PC 2007, Salesforce, MAC OS X, OS X, MS-DOS, Linux, UNIX
Hardware: Linksys Routers, Switches, Hubs, Notebooks, Workstations, Modems, Network Interface Cards, Graphics & Sound Cards, Hard Drives, Printers, Scanners
Software: Microsoft Active Directory, Microsoft Office Suite, Symantec Antivirus, McAfee Antivirus, Microsoft Server 2008/ 2012 R2, Norton Ghost, Acrobat Professional, Remote Desktop Client, Forefront Identity Manager (FIM)
Networking/Protocols: LAN/WAN, VPN, TCP/IP, DHCP, ICMP, IPV4, IPV6, ISDN, PBX, CAS, T1/E1, T3, PSTN, SS7. Knowledge of OSI Networking, Ethernet, ATM, VXML, Lucent Soft Switch, Cisco VoIP Gateways, Call Routing, CISCO BTS
Communications: VHF, UHF, HF, RF, SATCOM, COMSEC, SINGARS, ECMS, BFT
Languages: C, VB Script, SQL, PL/SQL, Hammer Visual Basic

Listing Technical Skills on your resume like the above example can take up a lot of space, but if it's relevant to employers that you have those skills (i.e. those skills were in the job description), then it's a good use of resume space.

For different examples of how to organize volunteer experience, awards, publications, organizational affiliations, or technical skills on your resume, review some of the resume templates in the Resources section at the end of this book.

Review, Review, Review

Since your resume is the first impression that a hiring manager has of you, make sure you proofread and spellcheck the document. I highly recommend that you also have several other people look over your resume to make sure you've caught any misspelled words or grammatical errors. There's nothing worse than listing "Detail-Oriented" as one of your Key Skills, only to misspell several words in your resume.

If you're not sure who to ask to review your resume, you can always connect with your local American Job Center. They will typically have an employment services representative who can review your resume for free. For information on how to locate your closest American Job Center, jump to the Resources section at the back of this book.

Chapter 3
Creating a Cover Letter

You've completed your resume and now you're ready to get started on the application—but not so fast! Before you start the application process, it's smart to create a cover letter that is tailored toward the specific position for which you're applying.

While there are some employers who don't bother to look at cover letters, the vast majority of employers view the applicant who includes a cover letter as more professional than those who don't. I have also worked with employers who don't bother to view an applicant's resume unless a cover letter is included. So, unless a position is closing in the next 10 minutes, it is well worth your time to create a cover letter tailored specifically to that position.

It is worth it to note, however, that many tech startups on the West Coast are not too keen on cover letters as they see them as an outdated. It's up to you how to proceed, but I tend to err on the side of caution and provide a tailored cover letter. After all, I'd rather have a hiring manager ignore a cover letter than have them not bother to read a resume because a cover letter wasn't included!

Okay, you get that it's smart to include a cover letter with your application, but you might be wondering what the purpose of the cover letter is in the first place.

The Purpose of a Cover Letter

Beyond just making you look a lot more professional than other applicants, cover letters serve two major purposes: 1) To provide information that doesn't belong in the resume and 2) To highlight specific experience or projects that make you the best candidate for the position. Let's break these down a little more with some examples.

Information That Doesn't Belong on the Resume

Occasionally, you may want to inform the hiring manager about a piece of information that makes you a better candidate for the position. Unfortunately, not all information belongs on the resume, which is why a cover letter can be helpful in delivering that information to the hiring manager before they've even read the resume. For example, you could use the cover letter to name-drop—that is, to let the hiring manager know that you're connected to a current employee of that company. Or maybe you were referred by a high-level executive at the company! A cover letter is the best place to provide that information to the hiring manager.

Other information you might include in the cover letter is that you are moving to the area soon. This can help maintain a hiring manager's interest when they notice that you live in a different state than where the job is located. Also, if you're telling the employer that you already plan to move to that region, then they won't automatically assume that you want them to pay for relocation expenses.

You can also use a cover letter to address any gaps in your employment history, though I only recommend doing this if the gap is really obvious and if you have a great, relevant reason for the break in employment. A good excuse for a gap in employment would be if you decided to focus on school to earn a degree relevant to the position. Or if you took a year off from work to travel the globe and experienced something or learned something during your travels that is relevant to the job.

Something else you can't really put in a resume but is perfect to include in a cover letter is your passion for that particular position or your interest in working for that specific company. Explaining that you've always admired the company's moral values or company culture can be an important point to convey to the hiring manager. It shows them that the position wouldn't be just another job for you, and that it would instead be a career with a company that you admire and want to work hard for in order to help the organization complete their objectives.

However, just like with the information in your resume, you want to make sure that anything you include in your cover letter is true. So, if you say that you admire the company's culture or their mission, then you'd better actually know what that mission or company culture is.

Explaining Why You're the Best Candidate

A cover letter shouldn't just consist of you rehashing your resume point by point. Don't forget, we're cutting the bullshit here. The employer already has your resume so you don't need to give them a play-by-play. Instead, the cover letter should highlight the top two to three reasons that you're the best candidate for the position. Though this usually means writing about positions or projects that are already listed in your resume, you won't just be listing those projects and hoping the employer understands why they're important. Instead, you're going to take the time to break down that specific experience and explain why it makes you a great candidate for a particular position.

Let me give you an example of what I mean. The following examples would appear in the second or third paragraph of a cover letter. (Don't worry, I'll be showing you how to write the whole cover letter in the next section.)

Job Description: Project Manager

The Project Method Company is seeking an experienced project manager to oversee the full life cycle of client projects. Must have experience in project oversight from the planning stages through project implementation and completion. Ideal candidates will be comfortable managing multiple projects simultaneously while delivering quality service to our clients in order to uphold the organization's stellar project management reputation.

The first example is for Candidate A applying to a Project Manager position. Candidate A saw the position and quickly typed up a cover letter which includes the sentence below as a standalone paragraph.

Project Manager Candidate A:

One reason I feel that I'm a great candidate for the Project Manager role at the Project Method Company is that I regularly managed projects while Regional Manager at XYZ Inc.

The second (better) example is that of Candidate B, who took the time to thoroughly read the job description. Candidate B noticed in the job description that the company is looking for someone with project management experience from the planning stages all the way through the execution phase. They also noticed that the job description specifically said they want someone who can help maintain the company's stellar reputation for handling project management contracts.

Project Manager Candidate B:

One reason I feel that I'm a great candidate for the Project Manager role is that, during my time as a District Manager at ABC Inc., I regularly managed the planning, execution, and review process for several multimillion-dollar projects simultaneously. With this experience, I feel that I would be well-positioned to maintain the Project Method Company's stellar project management reputation and thereby attract even more project management clients to the organization.

Okay, that last example was a little wordy, but it explained a little more clearly why that candidate would be a great fit and how they would apply their current skill set to the Project Manager position.

Let's look at another.

Job Description: Executive Assistant

We are looking for an experienced Executive Assistant who can provide administrative and secretarial services to our executive-level staff.

Required Qualifications:

- At least 2 years of experience assisting executive-level personnel
- Experience scheduling meetings and/or conferences
- Ability to collaborate with multiple organizations and offices to schedule meetings
- Experience creating and maintaining general office documentation

This first example is for Executive Assistant Candidate A who only focused on mentioning that they had some experience as an executive assistant.

Executive Assistant Candidate A:
In my role as an Administrative Assistant for the State, I provided direct assistance as an unofficial Executive Assistant to executive-level management.

The above is not a terrible sentence for a cover letter. At least Candidate A conveyed that they do have experience as an Executive Assistant, and hopefully that will explain why their resume might list them as an Administrative Assistant since that was their official job title. But you've got to admit that Candidate A's example is a little lacking. Especially once you compare it to Executive Assistant Candidate B.

In their cover letter, Candidate B worked in that they have experience as an Executive Assistant, but they also included that they possess some of the other skills that the company stated in the job description.

Executive Assistant Candidate B:
In my role as an Administrative Assistant for the State, I was selected above my peers to provide direct assistance for three years as an unofficial Executive Assistant for the Human Resources Department Director and the Assistant Director. I gained ample experience in scheduling high-level board meetings in collaboration with staff at other State department offices and regularly drafted state-level official documentation.

Notice how Candidate B not only worked in that they were selected above their peers to act as an Executive Assistant, they also made sure to include the specific experience they have that's relevant to the required experience in the job description.

If I had to choose between reading Candidate A's resume or Candidate B's resume, I'd most certainly pick Candidate B. Not only did they make it immediately clear that they possess the required qualifications that the company is looking for, but they also made it evident that, though their official job title might be Administrative Assistant for their role with the State, they actually served as an Executive Assistant for three years of that role.

How to Build a Cover Letter

Employers and hiring managers don't have a lot of time to spend pouring over your cover letter. That means you need to keep your cover letter short and to the point in order to be effective. I recommend keeping your cover letter to a maximum of one page. Any longer than that and the hiring manager is going to get bored and might not even bother to read your resume, as they might think that it is long-winded.

I like to break my cover letter up into specific paragraphs and usually end up with about four to five paragraphs including an introduction paragraph.

The Salutation/Greeting

When possible, it's good to address the letter directly to the hiring manager. Occasionally, an employer will list the name of the specific hiring manager for the role in the job description. This is fairly rare though, so you may have to do a little digging on the company's website to find a listing for their human resources manager.

If there isn't any contact information listed in the job description, you may consider reaching out to the company to inquire who is filling the role of hiring manager. When reaching out, simply let them know you plan to apply online but wanted to know who the hiring manger is so that you can address the cover letter to them.

Alternatively, if you can't find out a hiring manager or human resources manager's name, you could use the generic salutation, "To whom it may concern."

Introduction Paragraph

Though I call it a paragraph, the introduction is usually a one-line sentence where you express your interest in applying to the role. You'll be mentioning the specific position and company here, as well as the location of the role if the organization has multiple sites.

The introduction is also a great place to name-drop or otherwise let the employer know how you heard about the position.

I was excited to learn about the Logistics Manager position with XYZ Inc. from a previous co-worker, John Doe, who is currently the Vice President of Global Transportation at XYZ Inc. and am writing to express my interest in applying for the position.

If you're applying for a position in another state, you can use the introduction paragraph to let an employer know that you are relocating to their region.

I was excited to learn of the IT Specialist role with XYZ Inc. and am writing to express my interest in applying to the role, as I will soon be relocating to the region.

Second Paragraph

Here is where you jump into your first reason for being a great candidate for the position. This paragraph might mention experience, education, or a major project that makes you a great fit for the role. However, the piece that will grab the hiring manager's attention is providing an explanation for how that experience or education makes you a great candidate.

I feel that I'm a great candidate for the Logistics Manager position as I have over 12 years of experience managing logistics projects on a local, national, and global scale from my time as a Supply and Logistics Manager in the U.S. Army. During my service, I learned to quickly and efficiently respond to any issues in the logistics pipeline to ensure equipment and supplies arrived in a timely manner so that productivity was not affected. Applying this experience to the Logistics Manager role at XYZ Inc., I would be able to ensure limited interruptions to the company's logistics lifecycle.

Third Paragraph

Similar to the second paragraph, the third paragraph should be another reason that you're the best candidate for the role.

Another reason I feel that I would be a great fit for this role is that I recently completed an MBA with a concentration in Global Logistics. During my studies, I had the opportunity to complete an internship at BCY Corporation where I assisted the shipping department in increasing their speed of product delivery by 10%. I feel that by applying the concepts learned in my Master's program and internship, I'll be successful in improving XYZ Inc.'s productivity, personnel safety, and customer satisfaction.

Fourth Paragraph

This paragraph is what will set you apart from other candidates who have a similar experience or education as you. This is where you'll express what draws you to the position and/or the company. Alternatively, you can also explain why you're passionate about this field. Providing this information will make you a little more real to the employer and, as a result, they'll be more likely to actually remember you.

Lastly, I'm a passionate supporter of small businesses and would find it fulfilling to build a career with XYZ Inc. since it provides delivery services to small businesses across the globe.

If this section is very short (like the above example), then you might consider merging it with your fifth paragraph to shorten the cover letter. However, if this section is two to three sentences, then it's smart to leave it as a standalone paragraph.

Fourth/Fifth Paragraph

Tie it all together in the fourth/fifth paragraph by providing a quick review of your reasons for being the ideal candidate for the role.

With my extensive experience managing logistics projects, my education and experience improving an organization's productivity, and my passion for serving small businesses by providing top-notch logistics services, I feel that I could lead the Logistics Department at XYZ Inc. to exponential growth while increasing the satisfaction of logistics personnel.

The Closing

Lastly, you'll close the cover letter with a few short, to-the-point sentences.

I have attached my resume and applied through the online portal as directed. Please let me know if any other information or documentation is required.
I look forward to hearing from you.
Sincerely,
John Smith

Similar to the resume, double check all spelling and grammar before sending the cover letter to an employer. Since a cover letter is the first impression an employer will have of you, you want it to be a good one!

Want to see more cover letter examples? Jump to the Resources section for more examples of what you might say in a cover letter.

How to Submit a Cover Letter

Most of the time, you'll be given the option to upload your cover letter as a standalone document (that is, as a separate document from your resume) during the online application process. However, if you're applying online and there isn't an option to attach a cover letter, you might add your cover letter as the first page to your resume document so that the cover letter is the first thing an employer sees when they open your resume document.

If you are applying for a position by sending your resume to a hiring manager via email, you also can make the cover letter the body of the email and simply attach your resume to the email.

Chapter 4

The Application Process

Gone are the days of walking into a business, asking if they're hiring, and filling out a paper application. Though you can still walk into most service or retail industry locations to inquire if they are currently hiring, you'll most likely be asked to apply online or you'll be guided to an onsite computer used specifically for store applications. Regardless of your method of applying for a position, there are a few key pieces of information to know before you apply.

Online Applications

It is now standard practice for most employers to have you apply for their positions through an online portal or their career website. In fact, some employers require that you apply through their website in order to ensure that the hiring process is fair for everyone. With these employers, even if you know someone at the company, complete an interview, and get a job offer, you'll still be asked to officially apply through the online portal. So, regardless of who you know or the position level you're applying for, chances are that you're going to have to apply for a position online at some point. Before you start your application process, there are a few things to keep in mind.

What they don't tell you about online applications is that you'll basically be rewriting your resume in the employer's online application system. Some application systems will actually allow you to upload your resume at the beginning of the process and will then take the information from your resume and automatically populate sections of the online application. This is great if your resume is formatted in a way that is compatible with the application system. (Note: The resume template provided on my website and most of the resumes included at the back of this book are specifically formatted to be friendly to online application systems. The exceptions are the functional resume formats, which are labeled as such.)

Even if your resume is formatted in a way that is compatible with the application system, chances are that you'll still have to manually fill in or fix some of the information that failed to load correctly. Because resume formatting can affect the way information is populated in the application system, it's very common for information from the resume to populate in the wrong sections of the application or not show up at all.

If your resume is simply not compatible with the application system, you'll have to manually type the information into each section of the application system. The good news is that if you have a resume, you can simply copy and paste most of the information from your digital resume document. The bad news is that this means it will take a little longer for you to complete the application.

Application Process Best Practices

Most application systems require you to complete a registration to use their system. Usually this is just basic information (name, contact information, etc.). You'll also create a username and password for each application system. Though this may seem like a hassle, creating a username and password for the application system is useful, as it will allow you to come back later and finish your application if you need to take a break.

Keep it Professional

First, make sure that your username is professional. While it's possible employers or hiring managers never see this information, I recommend that you err on the side of caution and select a professional username. Something that includes your name would be appropriate. It's likely that the application system will make you use your email address as your username, which is another reason it's so important to have a professional email address.

Stay Organized

I mentioned back in Chapter 1 that it's important to keep a list of jobs that you apply for. Make sure to also include your username and password information on your list for each job as well. Some application systems will provide you with updates on your application's progress only if you log into their system.

Maintaining a list of the usernames and passwords for each position you apply for will make it easier to log into that application system in the future. This will be especially important if an employer calls you and asks you to upload any extra documents or information to their system.

Set Aside Enough Time to Apply

As mentioned above, you may have to manually fill in an entire application if the application system isn't compatible with your resume format or if the system doesn't give you the option to upload your resume. This means that completing an application for a single position could take some time. The typical job application takes one to three hours to fully complete, especially if you're tailoring your resume and a cover letter to the position.

Do not make the mistake of trying to complete a quick application during a 15-minute break at your current job. It won't be enough time to ensure that you've fully completed the application and that all the information is accurate and free of grammatical errors.

Instead, start your application when you know you'll have at least an hour or more to work on it. This will ensure that you don't feel rushed to finish the process and will keep you from making silly mistakes that could cost you the job. It will also allow you ample time to read through all the application's directions and possibly save you from missing an important step in the application process.

If you run out of time and have to choose between hitting the "submit" button or saving and coming back to finish it later, opt for saving your progress and resuming the application later. You want to make sure you're not only giving yourself time to complete the entirety of the resume, but also building in time to review all of the information and documentation before you submit the application.

The exception, of course, is if you're trying to apply for a position before it closes that day. In that case you need to complete everything that's required to apply, do a quick review, and then make sure everything is submitted before the deadline.

Have Your Resume in Front of You

When you start the online application process, it's smart to keep a copy of your resume handy, preferably in an electronic format. I like to have my resume document open in another window during the application process so that I can copy and paste information from the resume into the online application. This saves a lot of time, as copying and pasting keeps you from having to retype the information. Plus, it saves you from having to remember all your employment dates off the top of your head.

Have Your Cover Letter Ready

As mentioned in Chapter 3, a cover letter can make the difference between an employer even bothering to look at your application or moving on to the next candidate. It's smart to create a cover letter tailored toward the position before you start the application process. If you aren't given the option to upload a cover letter and there's something really important in the letter (like that you're planning to relocate to that area or you're name-dropping someone you know who works for that company) then one option is to make the cover letter the first page of your resume. Again, I only recommend doing this if there isn't an option to upload a separate cover letter document.

Have a List of Professional References

Employers expect you to have at least three to four professional references for whom you can share contact information including each reference's phone number and email. I've provided a professional references template on my website (https://www.evergrowthcoach.com/resources) if you want to get a feel for how a references page might look.

A professional reference should be someone who can provide positive feedback about your work ethic to a potential employer.

The best professional references to use are people you have worked with previously (a co-worker) or someone who has been your supervisor. Before applying for positions, reach out to your professional references and ask if it's okay for you to use them as a reference. This allows you to verify their contact information by asking what email and phone number they prefer you to list. If you don't have much work history, you may consider someone you worked with in a volunteer capacity. If you're a recent graduate or still in school, you can list a current or previous professor with whom you've established a positive relationship as a reference.

It is also acceptable to list a friend as a personal reference, but I highly recommend only listing one friend if you've never worked with them in a professional capacity. However, if you ever officially worked with that person at a company, you can list that friend as a professional reference rather than as a friend since they can explain what you're like at work to a potential employer. Even if you don't work with that person anymore and have simply remained friends, they could be considered a professional reference because you worked them at one time.

Avoid using any family members as references, as this can be seen as unprofessional. If you're applying for a position based on a referral from a family member who currently works at the organization, that should be mentioned in the cover letter instead. There is usually also a spot in the job application where you'll be asked how you heard about the position. That is a more appropriate time to mention you were referred by a family member who is a current employee of the company.

Just remember that the main thing you need from a reference is a positive review. This means that you should only list people that you know will say good things about you. If you know that a previous co-worker or supervisor will provide only negative feedback to an employer, then you should not use them as a reference.

When reaching out to a potential reference by email, include a copy of your resume so that they have a more well-rounded view of your employment history. If you're asking a professor for a reference, provide a brief summary to remind them of any projects or research you completed with them. Maybe you assisted them with research or ran a tutor group for them. Either way, it's good to provide a little information to jog their memories (and even better if you can tailor that paragraph toward something you did with them that is related to the job to which you're applying!).

Here is a great way to ask someone for a reference:

Hi John,

I hope you're doing well and that things are still going great at XYZ Inc.! I wanted to reach out as I'll be applying for engineering roles in the Indianapolis region and I wanted to see if you'd feel comfortable being listed as one of my work references. I've attached my current resume if that helps (and you'll see those projects we busted our butts on together listed under the XYZ position! Those were some interesting times, huh? I really appreciated all your support and hard work on those!).

If you feel comfortable with me listing you as a professional reference, please just let me know what phone number and email address you'd prefer me to use.

Thanks in advance and let me know if I can ever return the favor!

Notice how the above letter references a project that she worked on with the potential reference. If it's relevant to the positions to which she's applying, the reference is now more likely to mention that project when providing a reference to the potential employer.

Avoid Listing Previous Salaries in the Application

Some employers are now asking for information regarding previous salaries during the application process. It might seem innocent enough, but providing this information can actually pigeonhole you into making the same amount at this new company as you did at your last company. Basically, when an employer offers you a job with a lower than expected salary, they can then say to you, "Well, you were only making X amount at your last position, so this is what we're willing to pay you."

I have actually had this happen to me and was told the above statement, word for word, by a Human Resources (HR) representative when they offered me a position. Limiting pay based on your previous salary assumes that you'll be performing the same duties and responsibilities at your new position as those of your previous role. However, this is not usually the case. If you push back during the salary negotiation phase (which you will read more about in Chapter 8), and explain that the new role includes more responsibilities and a higher level of performance than your last position, you might end up getting a higher salary offer. Maybe.

The best option is to try and bypass this issue altogether. Rather than trying to convince HR that you're worth more than you previously made, I recommend not listing how much you previously made in the first place. If an application requires you to fill in a numerical value for the previous salary section (and won't allow you to move to the next screen without entering something in that box), then list the digit "0." Unless you listed that role as a volunteer position, the hiring manager will know that you were paid for that job and that you're simply choosing not to list how much you made.

Yes, there are some positions, like some state department jobs, that require you to list your previous salary, but the vast majority of hiring managers will simply overlook it if you choose not to list your previous salary in your application.

Avoid Listing Your Desired Salary

It's wonderful when an employer actually provides a salary range in the job description since this helps you determine if the role is the right fit for you financially. Unfortunately, most employers are rarely willing to provide that information upfront. Instead, many employers don't tell you a salary range until you get through the interview process. To add insult to injury, many employers will also require you to list your desired salary during the application process.

If you're confident that your desired salary range is in line with your experience and with the industry to which you're applying, then feel free to list your desired salary in the application. However, if you're not sure what salary you should be asking for, you're worried that you'll low-ball yourself, or you're concerned you might ask for too much and not get an interview, then I recommend not listing a desired salary in the application.

If the application system does not allow you to leave the desired salary blank, then list the digit "0." Don't worry. Employers know that you aren't saying that you'll work for free. By listing zero, all you're saying to the employer is that the salary will be discussed during or after the interview.

Note: If an employer lists a salary range in a position description, make sure that you're willing to accept a salary in that stated range. If you're looking for a position that pays more than the stated range, then I do not recommend applying for the position. Unless you know someone on the inside who has told you that the role will pay more, assume that the role will only pay within the salary range listed on the job description. If you apply, interview, and are offered the job at an amount within that range, you will only burn a bridge with that company if you demand an even higher salary.

I've Applied, Now What?

You've tailored your resume, created a cover that will capture the hiring manger's interest, and have officially applied for the job. Now what?

It can feel like employers are taking forever to get back to you regarding your application. Remember that it's likely that they have to comb through many applications to determine which applicants to bring in for an interview. Some organizations wait until a position officially closes before bothering to start interviewing candidates. Other organizations begin interviewing applicants as soon as eligible candidates apply. Regardless of how the organization works, there are a few things you can do to hurry the process along.

Two-Week Follow-Up

The best thing to do in order to find out what's going on with the job is to wait two weeks after you apply and then follow up with the organization regarding the job. This is another reason why it's so important to keep a list of the positions to which you apply. Make sure to add the date that you applied for the job to your list. You could even go ahead and list the date for when you should follow up with the company.

To follow up, see if there is a contact listed in the job description. Sometimes companies will include a specific HR representative or hiring manager associated with that position. Oftentimes though, you'll have to do a little sleuthing to figure out who you should follow up with. Try visiting the company's website to see if they have an email or phone number listed for their HR department. This can be a good place to start when trying to follow up.

Email or Call?

This, of course, depends on the type of contact information included with the job description or what kind of contact information you were able to find for the company. When possible, it's usually better to use a phone call to follow up. (I know, I'm not a huge fan of calling people either).

The reason you want to call rather than email is that you're more likely to get useful information from a phone call than from an email. The hiring process has a lot of rules and regulations to ensure that all applicants are given the same treatment. So, if you email and someone from that company emails you back saying that they think you're perfect for the job, that company has just shown you preferential treatment and there's a paper trail to document it. If you don't end up getting that job, you could go back to that person who told you that you were a shoo-in and demand to know why they told you that (after all, you have the email as evidence.) This is why most HR personnel don't provide a lot of specific information via email.

By calling the organization to inquire about the position, you're much more likely to get information regarding the position. You might find out when they plan to fill the role or when they plan to start interviewing candidates.

If email is your only option for following up, then it's still worth it to put in the effort to crafting a professional communication to inquire about the position and your application.

What should you say in your follow-up?

Regardless of whether you send an email or follow up with a phone call, your follow-up should include your name and the position to which you applied, as well as specifically mention that you're just following up on an application.

Here is a great script you can use for following up by phone:

Hi, my name is Jane Doe. I was just calling because I applied for the Marketing Manager position about two weeks ago and I just wanted to follow up to see if any other information is needed for my application.

Alternatively, you might specifically follow up about when they plan to interview for the position—especially if you've already interviewed for other jobs and received offers from them but are more interested in this role. In that case, a script like the following might be helpful:

Hi, I'm John Doe. I was just following up regarding an application I submitted for a Logistics Supervisor position. I wondered if I'm still being considered as a candidate and, if so, when the organization expects to bring applicants in for interviews.

Notice that neither of these scripts are demanding. They are cordial, provide pertinent information regarding the job you applied for, and get right to the point of what you're inquiring after. Also, keep in mind that one of the first suggestions of this book is to be nice to everyone. Always be cognizant of your tone and attitude when speaking to anyone from the organization, regardless of their status or position at the company. Every communication with the organization—whether by email or phone—should be professional and courteous.

In other words, if you call a company sounding annoyed that you haven't heard back from them, then they are unlikely to want to bring you in for an interview. After all, if you seem annoyed or demanding before they've even interviewed you, then they'd probably be concerned about what you would be like as an employee.

Chapter 5
Networking

The term "networking" seems to have gotten a bad rap in the last few years. Many people think networking requires schmoozing and pretending to be someone they're not in order to get their foot in the door with a company, but this doesn't have to be true! In fact, the more authentic you are, the more likely you are to connect with like-minded people who want you to work for their company.

Rather than approaching networking as an opportunity to pitch yourself, think of it instead as the act of making strong, professional connections with people involved in your industry. Keep in mind that people like to talk about themselves and will actually be more likely to remember you if your conversation allows them to relate something about themselves to you. Don't try to dominate the conversation with why you're such a great fit for their company. Don't keep circling back to your experience or accomplishments.

The most effective networking involves making real connections with people. Ask the other person questions about themselves or their careers. How did they get where they are today? What makes them enjoy working at their company? What are their hobbies outside work? If you focus more on learning about the other person (instead of trying to shove your career highlights down their throat), you'll more naturally identify similarities between yourself and the other person. Conversation will eventually drift to what you're doing professionally or what field you're trying to get into, and the other person will care more about your career goals because you showed that you care about theirs. This is how deeper connections are made.

While the best connections will be those you make in person, you can also make some great connections through online sites like LinkedIn (which you will learn more about in the next chapter.)

Who do You Network With?

It's a good practice to try to network with people who have some involvement with your industry or field of work. These could be people you've previously worked with or it could be someone you met at an industry-related conference. Another great place to network is career fairs, where you can build connections with potential employers as well as with other job seekers in your industry.

You may also find that connecting with people outside your industry can be useful as they may know someone hiring for your particular field.

Different Types of Networking

The main thing to keep in mind with networking is that, while your ultimate goal is to land a new position, you don't want to make networking all about asking for a job. Think about the last time someone suddenly reached out to you only to ask for something they needed. It was a little annoying when you realized that your old friend or previous co-worker was just reaching out to ask for a favor. It makes you feel a little used, right? If you didn't like the way that made you feel, then it's important that you not make people in your network feel that way either.

Networking with Friends or Previous Co-Workers

When you reach out to friends in your network, use the opportunity to catch up with them on a personal level. Ask questions. How have they been? How is their current job going? During the conversation, take note if there is anything they need that you can do for them. In the course of the conversation, let them know how you're doing and that you're actively seeking employment. Notice that this approach is quite different than asking them specifically for help finding a position.

If there is a position available at the company where your friend works, instead of asking them to refer you outright, use this conversation to learn more about the company and/or the position. Let your friend know that you saw an open position there and that you were thinking of applying but wanted to chat with them about the position or company first.

In most cases, your friend will provide you with information about the organization and/or the position and will likely offer to refer you for the position. If they don't say anything about referring you, then ask if it's okay if you use them as a professional reference when you apply.

Networking with Strangers

Keep in mind that the above suggestion is an acceptable way to proceed with a friend or previous co-worker who knows you well. It would not be as acceptable to reach out to a complete stranger in order to ask them to refer you for a position or to act as a reference. After all, if they don't know you or have never worked with you, then how could they possibly provide a positive reference for you?

When networking with a stranger in person or online, it's still good to get to know them. Ask them questions about their career, their company, or their position. If you're interested in a role with the company where they currently work, then express interest in that open role and ask them what it's like to work at that company.

Rather than asking outright for an favor from this person you've just met (in person or online), instead you're getting to know them and just asking for information to get a better idea of whether or not you should apply for a role. While your hope is that they'll offer to refer you for the position, you don't want to push your luck by outright asking for a referral.

Acing the Network Event

One of the most difficult parts of networking with strangers is the requirement to talk about yourself. What should you talk about? How much should you say? Rather than getting that deer-in-headlights look when you have to talk about yourself, prepare a short description of yourself and your current career goals. This short description is typically called an "Elevator Pitch" and is named as such because you should be able to get through it in the time it takes an elevator to make it to its destination.

Remember, it's best to build connections at a networking event by asking about the other person first. But eventually, the conversation will turn to you and why you're at the networking event, or the other person might ask you about yourself right off the bat. It's good to have an Elevator Pitch prepared so you'll know what to say about yourself.

Building an Elevator Pitch

Your personal Elevator Pitch will usually be a much shorter version of what you'd say during an interview when asked the dreaded tell-me-about-yourself question. The difference here is that your Elevator Pitch will also be a bit broader in scope. That way, should you ever randomly run into someone who asks what kind of work you're looking for (like, say, when you're in an elevator) you'll be ready with a concise, informative response.

A typical Elevator Pitch will sound something like this:

My name is John Doe and I specialize in global shipping and logistics. I've been with XYZ Inc. as a Global Shipping Director for 10 years and recently completed an MBA with a concentration in the logistical life cycle. I'm really interested in continuing my career in logistics and applying my experience at a larger organization.

Simple, clear, and straight to the point.

To build your Elevator Pitch, you first need to decide what field or industry you're targeting. Your opening line should include your name and the industry you've either been working in or the industry you are looking to transition to.

Next, mention one or two major highlights about your experience or education that are relevant to the field you're targeting. This may be that you recently graduated, completed an internship in your target field, earned a major certification relevant to your field, or have X years of experience in your target field.

Last, let them know what you want or what your interests are. In the above example, John Doe finished by letting his listener know that he hopes to continue his logistics career with a larger company. Maybe you're looking to transition to a new field by applying some recently acquired skills or training that's relevant to your target field. Alternatively, this last line could simply be letting your listener know that you're interested in learning more about their organization and the available positions.

Remember, keep your Elevator Pitch short, simple, and relevant to your target field or industry.

Preparing for a Job Fair

If you've ever attended a job fair, you know that they can be hit or miss on how successful they are in helping you land a position. However, a job fair is only as useful as you make it. If your preparation only entails showing up to a job fair dressed professionally with several copies of your resume ready to hand out to employers, then you're only about halfway ready and thus only have about a 50% chance of successfully connecting in a meaningful way with employers. To be 100% ready, you need to do a little more preparation before you arrive at the job fair.

Research and Make a List/Plan

First, research the employers who will be attending. There is usually a list of employers who plan to attend the event and sometimes that list will even give you an idea of what kinds of positions those employers are looking to fill. If the employer list does not include what positions they plan to fill, then hop on the computer and do a little research. Visit each employer's website and take note of the open positions listed on their company's career site. For each open position that you are qualified for and interested in, write down that position and note any questions you have about it and/or that company. This list of employers will be your plan for which booths you'll be visiting while at the job fair.

Most likely, not every employer will have positions that you are interested in. This means you've just cut down on how many employers you have to speak with at the job fair. However, it's still a good idea to pass by each employer's booth to make sure they aren't representing some new open position that hasn't made it to the company's career website yet.

If there is a company that you're really interested in working for but they don't have any positions posted that you're qualified for, it can't hurt to stop by their booth to chat with the representatives. Let them know you checked out their company website and didn't see any roles that were a great fit, but that you're really interested in working for the company and would love to get their business cards in case something opens up in the future.

Execute Your Plan

Now that you know which companies you want to connect with at the job fair and what questions you want to ask, let's move on to what you actually do during the event.

When you arrive at the job fair with your list of employers who you want to speak with, the first thing you want to do is to visit a booth for a company that you're not really interested in.

I know! It seems counterintuitive, but this is your practice session (just don't tell the employer that!). Doing this practice session with an employer you're not terribly interested in will let you get out any nervous jitters without hurting your chances with one of the companies on your list. Once you get through the practice session, you'll be more warmed up and ready to make a better impression on an employer who you're actually interested in working for. If you tend to get really nervous at these kinds of events, go ahead and speak with two to three employers who you're not interested in before speaking with any employers on your list.

Use a Tailored Elevator Pitch

Okay, you've gotten one or two practice sessions in and you're ready to speak with an employer who has a job listed that you're interested in applying for. This is where an Elevator Pitch will come in handy. Since you did your homework before the job fair and know which companies you're going to approach as well as which of their open positions interest you, make sure to have a tailored Elevator Pitch ready for them. To tailor your Elevator Pitch, let the employer know that you looked up their positions online and mention which position interested you the most and why it interested you.

For example:

Hi, I'm John Doe. I noticed your company has an open position for a Marketing Specialist. I graduated with a degree in Marketing two years ago and have been working in marketing since then, and I am really interested in your company and its current projects.

Notice how this Elevator Pitch is tailored toward a specific role at the company that caught your interest and relates why you're interested in that company. (The above example is actually pretty broad since it doesn't identify a specific company project that has caught your interest, so try to be a little more specific about why you are interested in the role or the company.)

With a tailored Elevator Pitch, you're much more likely to garner the employer's interest and they'll be more likely to remember you.

Be Prepared with Resumes

This is where those copies of your resume come in handy. Some employers will want to look over your resume and ask for it on the spot. It's better to be prepared and have a copy to give them that they can keep.

However, with the ease of today's online application systems, many employers won't bother to look over or take your resume. Instead, be prepared to be told by most employers that you should just go online to apply for their positions. Taking candidates' resumes results in a lot more paperwork for the recruiters to carry around. This is especially true if they are traveling from out of state for the job fair, as they'd have to lug a stack of resumes back to their office with them. I know, I know. It seems to defeat the purpose of an in-person job fair if the employer is just going to tell you to apply online and won't take your resume.

Just remember that a job fair is a networking event, which brings me to my next point.

Follow up, Follow up, Follow up

Don't expect to be offered a job at the career fair (though that does sometimes happen!). Instead, the name of the game is in-person networking and follow up. You're attending the job fair to let the employer know you're interested in a role with them. If they take your resume, great. If they don't take your resume and instead tell you to apply online, great.

Either way, make sure to collect business cards from the employers who have jobs you're interested in. Once you're out of eyesight from their booth, turn their business card over and write down something you learned during the conversation with them. When you get home, send an email to thank them for speaking with you at the job fair and mention at least one thing you discussed with them. This will help them remember who you are (since they will undoubtedly speak with many job seekers during the job fair). Attach your resume to the email as a PDF document and mention at the end of the email that you included your resume in case they wished to learn more about your experience.

Follow directions

If you were given specific directions by the employer for what you need to do next in order to be considered for a position, then you need to follow those directions! I cannot stress this enough. I've seen many applicants miss out on job opportunities because they couldn't be bothered to follow the directions that employers gave them during the job fair.

If you are told by an employer to apply for a position on their website, take the time to apply for the position as they directed before you email them to follow up. Then when you email the employer, you can thank them for the information they provided at the job fair, inform them that you applied for the position as directed, and let them know you attached your resume to the email as well in case they need it.

Your email might look something like the following example:

Good Afternoon Mr. Smith,

It was a pleasure meeting you today at the Fort Campbell Career Fair. I really appreciated learning more about XYZ Inc. and the available positions. I especially appreciated you taking the time to discuss the Logistics Manager role with me and detailing all the duties and responsibilities involved in that role.

Following your suggestion, I've completed the online application for the Logistics Manager position and have attached a copy of my resume for your perusal.

Please let me know if any other documentation or information is required in order to be considered for the Logistics Manager role.

Thank you again for your time,
John Smith

Just like with a cover letter, the simpler you make your email, the better. Employers don't have a lot of time to spend pouring over lengthy emails. Make their lives easier by getting straight to the point.

<u>Next-Level Networking</u>: Make the most of the job fair

When attending a job fair, most job seekers spend the entire event connecting only with the employers who are there representing organizations. While you definitely want to spend time networking with employers, it's also worth your while to connect with other job seekers. You never know who might be a good connection with a lead for a position.

So if you're waiting in a crowd of job seekers to speak with a specific employer, go ahead and introduce yourself to some of the other job seekers around you. If you have a LinkedIn account, ask if you can connect with them, and write down their name and email address so you can go online later and connect.

Chapter 6
LinkedIn

LinkedIn was specifically designed as a social networking website where people could connect with other professionals in their industry. Though the social media platform was originally designed for job seekers, it's since become useful for anyone who wishes to connect with other professionals in their industry, gain new skills from online professional development modules, or join group conversations or discussions with other professionals within their industry.

LinkedIn can still be a very useful tool during your job search, but it's only as useful as you make it. It does take a little time and effort to build a professional profile and develop a strong network of professional connections. If you don't intend to take the time to completely fill out your profile, add a professional picture, and monitor any messages you receive on the site, then I would recommend not having a LinkedIn profile at all. To an employer, a half-completed profile lacking employment history information or a picture suggests that you aren't actually that interested in pursuing new employment opportunities. It's an even worse impression if an employer reaches out to you via LinkedIn's internal messaging service and they don't get any kind of response from you.

Before you sign up for a free LinkedIn profile, decide how much time you want to put into building a professional social media profile on the site. After all, your LinkedIn profile will usually be one of the first impressions you make on an employer. You want to make sure it's a good one!

Creating a Professional Profile

You've decided to build a professional LinkedIn profile—great! Once you register with the site and verify your email address, you'll be prompted to start filling in information for your profile. Notice that, just like a resume, your LinkedIn profile is broken down into sections. Much of the information such as previous employment history, education, and volunteer experience can be copied directly from your resume. However, there are some sections that you'll want to make a little different than your resume and other sections that you may not have on your resume at all, like an interests or hobbies section.

Another similarity between your LinkedIn profile and your resume will be the use of keywords. This is especially important for your LinkedIn profile as recruiters and hiring managers can search LinkedIn using keywords to find potential employees to fill their open roles. So, if you're looking for a role in a specific field or industry, then you'd better make sure the keywords specific to that field are sprinkled throughout your LinkedIn profile.

Since most of the LinkedIn profile parallels a resume, I'll focus only on the sections that will be different from a resume. If you want more information on how to flesh out your employment history using keywords, I recommend jumping back to the resume section of this book, which provides you with step-by-step instructions for how to identify industry-specific keywords.

Profile Picture

Though it is ultimately up to you whether or not to upload a picture for your LinkedIn profile, I highly recommend having one since most people will not bother connecting with you if you don't have a profile picture. Recruiters and hiring managers will be much less likely to bother viewing your LinkedIn profile if you don't have a picture, since that looks like you're not really that interested in the job search.

But what picture should you upload? Though there are photography services out there that specialize in creating professional headshots for LinkedIn and other professional websites, you don't have to use those services to create a professional picture.

Instead, simply put on the same type of clothes you would wear to an interview (If you're not sure what to wear for an interview, jump to Chapter 7 for suggestions.) Find a neutral background for your picture (a neutrally painted wall is fine). Then ask a friend or family member to take a few pictures of you from the chest or shoulders up (whichever you feel more comfortable with). It's a good idea to take several pictures so that you can choose the best one to use on your profile.

If you have a selfie stick, you might be able to get away with taking the picture yourself. Just make sure it's not evident that you're the one taking the picture. Avoid taking pictures in bathroom mirrors since you can usually tell this is where the picture was taken. Also, it's best to use a whole new picture for your LinkedIn profile rather than trying to pull a picture off one of your other social media sites (unless you have a professional picture on those sites.)

Your profile picture should consist SOLELY OF YOU. This is not the time to upload a picture of you and your spouse, family, significant other, dog, etc. Do NOT upload a picture where you've cropped other people out. We can tell you did this. Veterans: Do NOT upload your DA photo. You want civilian employers to be able to picture you at their company, which they can't do if you give them a picture of you in military regalia.

Headline

After your profile picture, the second most important thing on your LinkedIn profile is your Headline. This is the short one-liner that pops up directly underneath your name. When you request to connect to other professionals on LinkedIn, your headline is the second thing those professionals see after your picture. It's also the first thing that hiring managers or recruiters look at, and when those same recruiters search for potential job candidates, the system will use your headline as part of their keyword search.

Do not make the mistake of simply listing your current job title for the headline. In fact, since you now know that keyword searches performed by recruiters take the headline into account, you should make sure your headline has some major keywords for your field listed.

As mentioned in the resume section, keep in mind that keywords are duties, responsibilities, or education/training that pertains to the position. Recruiters and hiring managers are not going to search for fluff terms like "top performer," "results-driven," "professional," or "successful" in a keyword search. Try to avoid using these fluffy filler words in your profile. Instead, use keywords that match up to the specific role in your field.

To figure out what keywords you should use in your headline and LinkedIn profile, jump back to the section on identifying industry keywords in Chapter 2. Check out the examples below to get an idea of how to build a useful headline that will populate in an employer's job applicant search when they use keywords.

Example 1: Logistics/Logistics Manager
    Field/Industry Keywords: Logistics Manager; Global Logistics; Shipping; Distribution; Logistical Lifecycle; Supply Chain Manager; SAP
    Potential Headlines: "Global Logistical Lifecycle Manager," "Shipping & Distribution Logistics Manager," or "Supply Chain Manager & SAP Expert"

Example 2: Human Resources/(Entry-Level) Human Resource Specialist
    Field/Industry Keywords: Human Resources; Personnel Services; Administration; Payroll; Benefits; Employee Services; Talent Acquisition; Recruiting
    Potential Headlines: "Human Resources Specialist & Benefits Coordinator," "Payroll & Benefits Human Resources Specialist," "Human Resources & Talent Acquisition Specialist"

Still stuck trying to figure out a great headline for your LinkedIn profile? Try going to LinkedIn and running a search to see what other professionals in your field have used as headlines. You can search by typing the name of your field (i.e., "Human Resources") or position (i.e. "Project Manager") right into the search bar on the top left-hand side of the LinkedIn homepage after you sign in.

See a great headline someone else in your field is using? See if you can modify it slightly to fit you and your experience.

Summary

There is also a summary section on LinkedIn and, while you can use the summary from your resume, it is recommended that you make the summary section on LinkedIn a little less rigid than the summary in your resume.

One way to make this section less formal than the one in your resume is to use "I" statements. You might even create a lengthier version of the "Elevator Pitch" you created earlier in the networking section (Chapter 5).

Your summary might look something like this:

As an Organizational Development Manager, I'm a big believer in harnessing innovation to tackle organizational challenges. I also find it extremely important to identify issues at all levels of an organization by communicating directly with personnel across all departments to listen to their concerns and hear their suggestions for organizational or process improvements. Through such open communication, I have been able to achieve production improvements of up to 50% while simultaneously bolstering employee satisfaction, which directly resulted in a 25% increase in customer satisfaction. I also have ample experience in creating internal employee development programs as well as internal management pipelines to give top personnel the opportunity for career progression. While sales and production numbers are important, I find that the best methods for increasing these numbers is by improving the organization from the ground up by starting with employee satisfaction and morale.

Just like a resume, you'll want to make sure the summary section contains content that is relevant to the field or position for which you want to apply.

Skills & Endorsements

Though some will argue about the benefits of this section, it can't hurt to take the time to fill in the Skills section of your LinkedIn profile. Always select skills that are relevant to your field. For example, as a career coach, a useful skill for me to list is that of Career Coaching. You can list a ton of skills in this section, but currently you can only select three to be listed on your profile page (people can still view your other skills, but only if they click on the skills section of your profile to expand the skills list.) Make sure to choose the most relevant skills to your field to list as your top three skills.

Once you've listed some skills, your LinkedIn connections will then be able to "endorse" you for those skills. That is, they'll be able to click on that skill and rate your ability in that area. The idea here is that endorsements are supposed to show credibility. If many people endorse you for possessing a skill, then it seems more likely that you actually possess that skill and you aren't just throwing it in your profile because it's a keyword for your field.

Building up endorsements for skills is a sort of "give to get" system. When you connect with current or previous co-workers, endorse some of their skills and they'll be more likely to give back by endorsing you for your skills.

Recommendations

The recommendations section of your LinkedIn profile is a great way to show employers what a great co-worker or employee you are. Instead of having to wait to call the recommendations you provide in an application, employers can go straight to your LinkedIn profile and read what others have to say about working with you. It can only help you if you have rave reviews from co-workers or managers at your previous places of employment!

Similar to the skills section, recommendations tend to work on a "give to get" system. Once you connect with current or previous co-workers, create a thoughtfully written recommendation for them. Take some time to do this right so that they will be more likely to reciprocate in kind. Make sure your recommendation for them is free of spelling and grammar errors.

A great thing about recommendations is that you can review any recommendations you receive before allowing them to be posted on your LinkedIn profile.

Building Connections

Once you've developed a professional LinkedIn profile, it's time to start building those professional connections in order to get the most from the site. The main idea for LinkedIn is to use it as a tool to connect online with people you've actually met or have connected with in real life in order to create a professional network.

Start with People You Know

The quickest way to build up your connections on LinkedIn is to allow the site to view the contacts from your email address book. (LinkedIn will usually automatically ask you if you would like to complete this step to find more contacts.) The site will search through your email address book (if you allow it to) and automatically review all your contacts to see if those contacts have accounts on LinkedIn. If those contacts have LinkedIn profiles, you can have the system send a LinkedIn connection request to those contacts. This will allow you to more easily connect with co-workers, old classmates, or family members (as long as you have their email listed in your email address book.)

Alternatively, you can complete a manual search for people you know by typing their names into the search bar on LinkedIn (usually located on the top, left-hand side of the screen.) Once you find the person you're looking for, you can click the "Connect" button to send them a connection request.

However, remember that the system is set up for connecting with people you know in real life. To make sure you're not trying to connect with random strangers, the system might ask you to provide an email address for the person you're trying to connect with. Basically, it's making you prove that you actually know that person in real life. If you know that person's email address and can provide it to LinkedIn to prove you actually know that person, then the system will send them a connection request. That person will have to accept the connection request before you're fully connected.

Once they accept your request, you are then considered 1st level connections because you are directly connected to them. All of their connections are considered 2nd level connections to you since you are connected to them through this other person.

Confused yet? Let's look at an example in order to clear things up.

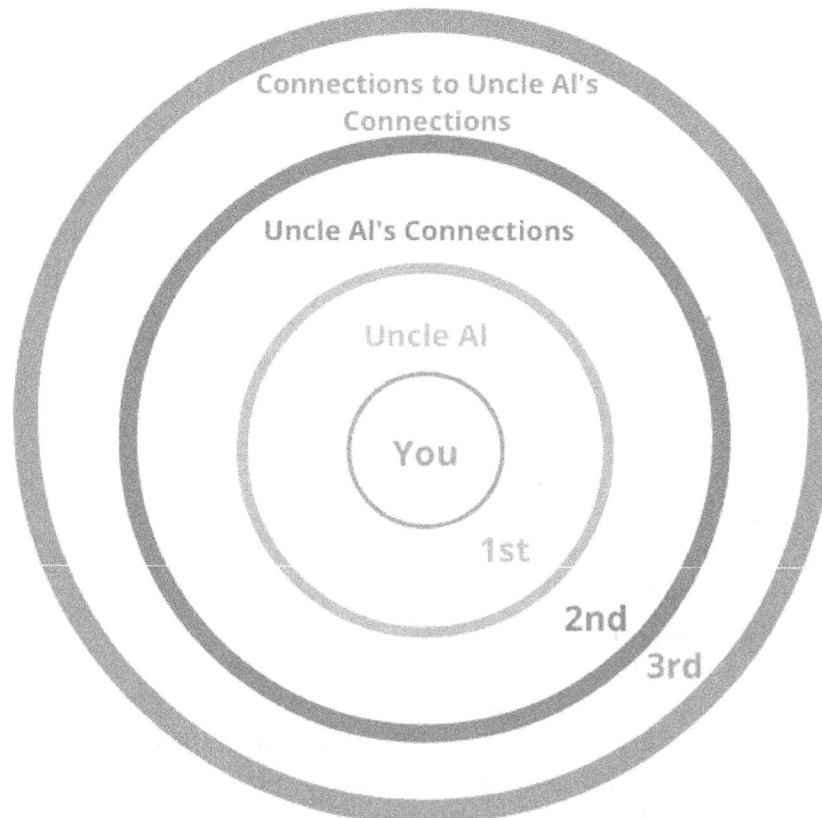

Example of How LinkedIn Connections Work

Let's say that you let the system access your email address contacts and the system sees that you have an email saved in your address book for Uncle Al. The LinkedIn system will then ask you if you want to send him a connection request. You send the request; Uncle Al accepts your connection (he's so glad you've decided to join this century and start a LinkedIn profile!) Now you are connected to Uncle Al.

Once connected with Uncle Al, he is then considered a 1st connection of yours because you are directly linked. This also means that all of the people he's currently connected to become 2nd connections to you and you can send them a connection request (without providing an email address) since you're connected to them through Uncle Al.

As you can guess, building out your connections on LinkedIn can initially feel a little tricky since you're limited to connecting only with people you actually know. However, over time it is possible to build up a robust network of professionals within your industry who you've never met.

Start with the professionals you know from your industry, such as current or previous co-workers or professors from college. Once connected to them, you'll gain access to their connections and will be able to send a connection request to the people they know. LinkedIn now also offers the option of sending a short note with your connection request. I highly recommend creating a note when attempting to connect with other professionals in your industry who you've never met. Keep it simple; let them know you have a mutual connection and that you would like to connect with them since they work in the same industry as you.

Connect with Acquaintances

The next step to building your LinkedIn network is to request to connect with the employers and other applicants you meet at job fairs. Again, send a short note to remind them how you met and that you'd like to connect as you are building up your professional network. Remember that once you connect with these professionals, you'll then have access to their professional connections.

Join LinkedIn Groups

The next method for building out your professional network on LinkedIn is to join some LinkedIn groups that are related to your profession. Groups on LinkedIn are a sort of separate area where professionals in the same industry can share information or articles related to their field. You can search for specific types of groups using keywords from your industry or you can start your own group if you don't see one for your particular field. While many groups are open and can be joined with just the click of a button, some want to make sure they are allowing only professionals within a particular industry to join. For these more particular groups, you may have to wait until an administrator for the group grants you access.

Once you've joined a few groups related to your profession, you'll be able to see the content posted by other group members. If you see professionals posting information within these groups that you find helpful, consider sending them a connection request. Again, send a note with your connection request to let them know you're part of the same group and that you've appreciated the information they've provided.

As you develop your professional network on LinkedIn, don't be surprised if people you don't know reach out to you and request a connection. It is completely up to you if you want to connect. Before I connect with someone I don't know, I usually view that person's profile to see if we share any professional similarities. It's okay to connect with strangers on LinkedIn, but it will be the most beneficial to you if you're connecting with professionals who are in your industry.

Note: Many entrepreneurs and small business owners have taken to using LinkedIn as a method for connecting to potential customers. They will send you a connection request and upon connection, immediately send you a message about their services and products. I tend to either ignore these messages or send a polite, "No thanks," message, but I usually keep them as a connection. However, with the more persistent spammers, I will remove them as a connection. It's up to you how you want to proceed in these cases.

What to Avoid on LinkedIn

Though Spammers (see Note above) are annoying, they are not half as annoying as people who don't use LinkedIn appropriately. Again, it's important that you remember that LinkedIn is a professional networking social media platform. To avoid being inappropriate on LinkedIn, a good rule of thumb to follow is that if you wouldn't say or do something in a professional work setting, that behavior is not appropriate on LinkedIn.

Just to make sure we're all on the same page, here are a few specific suggestions to follow while using LinkedIn.

Do Not Use LinkedIn as a Dating Site

This means, do not connect with someone and then immediately message them with inappropriate comments about how they look. It doesn't matter if you think it's a compliment. It's inappropriate. And prefacing your statements with, "I know this isn't a dating site, but…" doesn't excuse the behavior. This behavior is NOT professional. Anyone who thinks these kinds of comments are acceptable at work should have a long talk with their HR department.

If you are on the receiving end of this kind of behavior, immediately remove your connection with this person. No matter what their profession or position is, they are not worth being connected to.

Do Not Post Political or Religious Content

Unless you work in politics or religion, it's best to not post your political or religious opinions on your LinkedIn profile. Remember that employers will look at your profile and can see everything you post. It's also important to note that everyone can see the comments you make on LinkedIn. So even if you didn't post something, if you commented on it or "liked" it, then employers can see that and are very likely to make hiring decisions based off those comments. Of course, you won't know that's why you weren't hired. You'll just never hear back from those employers.

Remember, if you wouldn't talk about something at work or in an interview, then it doesn't belong on LinkedIn.

Don't Spam other People

Think about how annoying it is to get unwanted messages from people trying to sell you something. Recruiters and hiring managers feel the same way when you message them to ask, "Do you have any jobs for me?"

Instead, you need to do the legwork of researching positions at their company, and then apply online through the normal channels. Only then should you reach out to the recruiter to let them know you applied. You're not asking for an interview—you're just letting them know you applied to a specific position at their organization.

Don't Argue with People in Comments

Arguing with people in the comments section on any social media website is about as effective as spitting into the wind. You'll only get angry and you will never change the other person's opinion. You are, of course, entitled to your opinion, but once you've commented on a topic, move on. Remember, potential employers can see your comments and it's not a great impression of you to employers if all they see you doing is arguing with other commenters.

LinkedIn can be a truly helpful tool to develop your professional network. Just make sure you're using it in a professional manner so as to avoid turning off potential employers and other professionals in your industry.

Chapter 7

Interview Preparation

Before getting into the employment services industry, I used to totally wing it in interviews. No preparation, no reviewing the job description—basically, I made sure I showed up on time, knew the name of the person who was supposed to interview me, and answered their questions with enthusiasm and interest. That was fine for interviewing for part-time service jobs during high school and college, but I quickly learned that using the wing-it method after graduation to get a role related to my career was not going to cut it.

You see, employers hiring for long-term, career employees don't just want someone they can have a pleasant conversation with (though it helps). They want someone with substance who requires minimal training, shows passion for the position or industry, and can speak knowledgeably about the responsibilities of the role. If I had realized this and put some effort into preparing for interviews, I could have had so many more job offers after college!

Regardless of how confident you are in your interview skills, it's worth it to take the time to prepare. After all, there is always room for improvement regardless of how amazing you are. Also, you don't want to put all that effort into the resume and application process, then not bother to prepare for the interview. It's like training for months to qualify for a marathon, then deciding to just stop training a few months before the race but still expecting to win. I guarantee at least some of the other applicants for the job are practicing and preparing to knock the interview out of the ballpark, so you'd better do the same if you expect to compete with them.

And don't make the mistake of believing the myth that you can't prepare for an interview since you don't know what questions the interviewer(s) will ask. While it's true that you are unlikely to know exactly what questions will be asked, there are a few basic questions that most interviewers will ask in some form. We'll go over those in this chapter and more importantly, review what the interviewer is really looking for in an answer. We'll also review how to use the job description itself to prepare for the interview process.

But first, we're going to go over some basic information regarding interviewing including general tips, the different types of interview styles, what to expect for each type of interview, and basic interview do's and don'ts.

General Interview Tips

I could probably write an entire chapter (or book!) solely on general interview tips, but since we're cutting the bullshit here, I'll keep these tips to just a small section.

Bring a Pen and a Notepad to the Interview

Though you don't have to take notes during an interview, it's better to be prepared just in case. After all, if you're asked an interview questions that has multiple parts, it can be useful to jot down some notes to remind you of each part of the question in order to ensure you fully answer it.

It's also useful to have a notepad handy in case the interviewer doesn't have a business card but provides you with an email address to write down; that way, you can still follow up with a thank-you letter after the interview.

Avoid Mentioning an Upcoming Vacation

Broaching the topic of vacation time for which you'll already need days off before you've been offered the job will not leave a very good impression on an interviewer. Instead, wait until you're offered the position.

Always Try to Answer the Interview Questions

Much like not having any questions to ask the interviewer can be the kiss of death, telling an interviewer that you don't have answer for their question is a terrible way to miss out on a position. Unless the interviewer is asking you an illegal question (Such as: Do you have any kids? What's your religious affiliation? Do you have a disability?), then you should do your best to provide an answer.

Sometimes this might mean providing as close of an answer as you can. For example, if an interviewer says, "Tell me about a time you argued with a supervisor." Then you might say something like, "I don't believe I've ever actually *argued* with a supervisor, though I have had disagreements with a previous supervisor. For example…" and then go on to provide a STAR answer (We'll cover STAR answers soon!) that explains your disagreement and what you did about it.

Stall for Time When Needed

Repeat the question out loud or say something like, "That's a great question." Though these strategies only buy you a few seconds, it may be enough time to come up with an answer.

Types of Interviews

There are many different types of interviews available to hiring managers nowadays, so it's good to be familiar with what you might encounter and run some practice sessions with the different types of interviews to prepare.

Single Interviewer

The easiest type of interview is a one-on-one, face-to-face interview in which you can focus on providing answers to just one person's questions. The single interviewer session will usually allow an applicant to get to know the interviewer a little bit better, as the interviewer is likely to provide more specific information when no one else is around.

Multiple Interviewers

An interview session in which there are multiple interviewers, also known as a panel interview, can feel a little more intimidating. The main thing to keep in mind during this type of interview is that, regardless of which interviewer asks the question, make sure that you give the answer while looking at each of the panelists/interviewers in turn. Fight the urge of only looking at one interviewer while providing your answers. It can make other interviewers feel left out, or worse, give them the feeling that you are marginalizing or ignoring them for some other reason.

Multiple Interview Candidates

Another interview possibility is that of completing an interview with several other applicants at the same time. This can feel quite confusing. The best method here is to make sure you don't hog all the attention by trying to be the first to answer every question. Make sure to answer one or two questions first to show you're not intimidated or shy, but also give others the chance to be the first to provide an answer to questions. If your answer is similar to someone else's, say so, but also see if you can add a little more depth or a personal example to the answer.

Interview Modes: In Person vs. Over the Phone vs. Video Interviewing

While most employers still prefer to hold interviews within their office, many are opting to hold initial interviews over the phone or via video. Some use these phone or video interviews as a screening process to remove unqualified candidates before moving to a second round of interviews that are held in person.

It's very important to practice before an interview that will be over the phone or via video and to make sure you practice in that same interview mode. This way you feel more comfortable with that mode of interviewing AND you will be better able to identify any issues you may encounter during the real interview.

For example, when speaking by phone, some applicants tend to make an audible noise while thinking of how to answer a question. This is fine during an in-person interview since the interviewer can see your face and therefore knows that you are thinking. However, during a phone interview, it can become quite distracting (or even annoying!) to an interviewer.

This is also true of video interviewing when it comes to facial expressions. Some applicants forget that during a video interview, the employer can see the applicant's face. I've seen applicants make some interesting facial expressions on a video interview that they would never have made in an in-person interview. It's easy to forget that the interviewer can see your facial expressions when you're interviewing from the comfort of your own home, so make sure to practice interviewing via video with someone who will give you candid feedback not just on your answers, but also on your demeanor.

Another up-and-coming interview trend for screening out unqualified candidates is that of requiring candidates to complete video-recorded interviews using an automated system.

For these video-recorded interviews, the candidate will typically receive a link to an online system through which they will complete the recorded interview. Most of these interviews have a screen that provides the interview question and a timer so that the applicant will know how much time they have left to finish their answer to that question.

If you receive an invitation for a video-recorded interview, I highly recommend using a free website to practice answering general interview questions while being recorded before committing to the real interview.

Jump to the Resources section for a list of websites that provide free video-recording interview practice.

Interview Do's and Don'ts

I hate to use the words "never" or "always" when providing suggestions for the employment process, as there is inevitably an exception to most rules. However, when it comes to interviewing, it's good to try to follow these suggestions since they come directly from hiring managers and human resources representatives. If you feel like you're the exception to one of these rules, then I recommend running it past an employment services professional to make sure it's actually acceptable in an interview (and isn't the thing that's will keep you from getting the job!)

Do's

Do Bring Three Hardcopies of Your Resume and Three Hardcopies of Your Professional References

Some interviewers might never ask you for a hardcopy of your resume or references. If they don't ask for it, then you don't need to give them a hardcopy—but you should still bring three copies of both the resume and references to the interview anyway.

This may seem like overkill. After all, you applied online and the interviewer should have reviewed an electronic copy of your resume before the interview, right? Unfortunately, that is not always the case. Some interviewers don't bother looking at resumes until the candidate is in front of them. This could work to your advantage if you've made updates to your resume—especially if the changes show you're a stronger candidate for the job. If that is the case, make sure to mention to the interviewer that you've made those updates to your resume before handing it to them.

Another reason to bring a copy of your resume is that I have seen too many instances of someone being asked to interview a candidate when the actual interviewer couldn't make it to work that day. This means that the fill-in interviewer might not even have access to a copy of your resume.

Why three copies? If your interview is with more than one person, then bringing more than one copy of your resume will show forethought on your part and that you put in the effort to be prepared.

Do Dress Appropriately for the Interview

While it's usually appropriate to dress up for an interview, it also depends on the type of position you're interviewing for. If you're interviewing for a position within the skilled trades industry, most employers will tell you what to expect for an interview—especially if a portion of the interview will include you performing a task to show your abilities. Some skilled trade employers will suggest you bring work clothes to change into for that portion of the interview, or they will suggest you wear your work clothes for the entire interview process. If the skilled trade employer doesn't mention what to wear, it's acceptable to ask. You can say something like, "I was wondering if there will be a portion of the interview where I'll be showing my skills in welding and if so, should I bring a change of clothes that are safe to weld in or would you prefer I simply wear those clothes to the interview?"

For most interviews, the best practice is to dress up. This usually means some variation of a suit. After all, you can always dress down at the interview by removing your jacket or blazer. Try to stick to neutral colors like black, navy, or grey. It's not wrong to wear a different color than those three, but unless you're interviewing for a position in the fashion industry, you want the interviewer's attention to be on your interview answers and not on what you're wearing.

If you're applying for a position and you think that a suit may be too dressy for that particular industry or position, then another option would be khaki pants and a professional button-down shirt or blouse.

If you're strapped for cash and don't currently have any appropriate interview attire, check out the Resources section at the end of this book for financial assistance for interview attire.

Do Smile or Show Your Positive Personality or Humor (as Appropriate) During an Interview

As a woman who hates being told, "You should smile more," I really dislike giving this advice to others. However, I'm not suggesting that you smile throughout the interview (regardless of topic) as doing that might lower the interviewer's impression of you regardless of gender.

Instead, I'm aiming this advice to those who, when nervous, tend to clam up and become very serious. Remember that part of purpose of the interview is to see if you're a good fit for the culture of that company and its office. You should always be yourself, but if you know that you get nervous in interviews and don't show your true self (the self that would get you the job) then try practicing interviewing with a friend, family member, or employment services professional in order to work on getting past that nervousness.

One of the major groups that I tend to give the "smile more" advice to are my veteran clients. If you're a veteran, you might fall into the habit of treating an interview like a performance board evaluation where smiling is not exactly…smiled upon. If you're a veteran transitioning to your first post-military position and are interviewing for the first time, either do some interview practice with non-military friends or family members or get assistance from someone who has transitioned from the military and has already held a position in the civilian world. I've seen some veterans miss out on positions because they appeared too "militant" in the interview.

Do Arrive to the Interview 15 Minutes Early

You want to make a good first impression during your interview, which means being on time. To make sure nothing keeps you from being late, double check your travel route for getting to the interview and add at least an extra 15 minutes to your travel time. This will usually ensure that you won't be late.

That 15-minute window is a good rule of thumb for when to arrive to an interview. It shows that you're excited about the position and care about being on time for the interview. Keep your early arrival just to 15 minutes though, as arriving too much earlier than that can actually be seen as annoying to company staff.

Do Have a Salary Range in Mind in Case You Receive an Offer

Every company is a little different in when they reveal the salary range for a position. Some companies provide salary range information in the job description, some mention it in the first screening interview, some only reveal it after an offer has been made, and some never tell you a range at all and instead simply ask you in the interview what salary you're looking for.

Regardless of the information you do or don't have about the position's salary range, it's still a good idea to have a minimum salary range in mind that you'll accept as well as your ideal salary range for that position. Having these numbers in mind will keep you from being blindsided should you receive a job offer in the first interview and be expected to accept or decline a specific salary. To learn more about how to determine that amount, check out Chapter 8.

Do Follow up with a Thank-You Email After the Interview

This might seem old school, but following up with a thank you letter within 24 to 48 hours of the interview can make you stand out from other candidates as a professional. It also shows that you're truly appreciative for the interview opportunity. I do recommend using email rather than snail mail as you don't want the thank-you letter to get lost in the mail room and not end up on the right desk.

Keep your email short and sweet—this is not the time to provide a better answer to an interview question you flubbed. The email should be used to actually thank the interviewer, and it is also an opportunity for you to remind them of something you discussed during the interview (preferably something that coincidentally makes you a great candidate for the position or showed your passion for the job). Don't worry, there are examples of thank-you letters at the end of this chapter.

Don'ts

Don't Bring Anyone Else to the Interview

The interview is about you and your ability to perform the job, so you shouldn't be taking anyone else to the interview with you. If you bring your parent or significant other to an interview (yes, this has happened), then you're signaling to the interviewer that you can't interview by yourself and therefore won't be able to handle the job by yourself. It's also important not to bring your children to an interview either as that indicates that you won't be able to find childcare if offered the job. This is the time to splurge for a babysitter or take advantage of local childcare resources if available.

Don't Harass the Interviewer After the Interview (but do Follow up)

It's good to be excited about a potential position, but calling or emailing the company too much after an interview is a big turn-off for hiring managers. The generally accepted guidelines are to follow up the interview with a thank you email within 24 hours of the interview, and then to call or email two weeks after the interview if you haven't heard back from the company. I have seen candidates miss out on positions because they followed up with a company too often and made themselves into a nuisance.

The best rule of thumb is, at the end of the interview, to ask what the next steps are and then follow those steps. If that means waiting three weeks to follow up with the interviewer instead of two because they said it would take three weeks to reach a decision, then wait three weeks to follow up.

Don't "Ghost" an Employer

I know, I know. This is one of the most widely complained about issues for job applicants since some employers don't follow up with you after you've applied or interviewed for a position. This is known as ghosting. However, just because some employers ghost you, doesn't mean you should do the same to other employers.

If you decide not to accept a job offer or not to move forward in an interview process for any reason, it's best to be upfront with the hiring manager and let them know you're no longer interested in the role. Try to be as honest as possible about your reasons—after all, if it's because of a low salary or something else that could be modified, you might find yourself with a more desirable offer from the company after being honest.

Don't Be Rude to Other Candidates

Occasionally it does happen that you meet another candidate interviewing for the same position as you. This is not the time for psychological games. Instead, be polite to them. If you're rude and the company hires both of you, then you don't want to accidentally have started out on the wrong foot with a co-worker before you've even started the job.

Also, meeting someone else while interviewing is a potential networking opportunity with a professional who is clearly in the same industry as you! So be cordial, get their name, and then follow up with them via LinkedIn. Even if they get the job and you don't, they may have other suggestions for roles at other companies you do not know about. Or they could end up being a great referral for another job that opens up with that company in the future.

Don't Talk Negatively About Previous Employers or Co-Workers

When asked why you're leaving a position or why you left a company, it may be tempting to discuss how terrible a supervisor was to you or how badly an organization might have treated you as employee, but resist that temptation. An interviewer doesn't want to hear you complain about the drama from an old job. In fact, if you do complain, they'll wonder what you'd say about their company if they were to hire you.

Instead, try to focus on the skills or experience you gained from the position. When they ask why you left, explain that it was a "great opportunity in which I learned (insert skill here), but since I was there for X amount of years, I really felt it was time for a new challenge… which is why I'm so excited about this role."

Even if the interviewer asks you a situational question such as, "Tell me about a time you didn't get along with a supervisor or co-worker," it's still best to avoid being overly critical of previous co-workers or supervisors. Use the STAR method (see Situational Questions and STAR Answers later in this chapter) to give a short version of the situation, then explain what you did to try to remedy the disagreement or issue.

Don't Tell the Interviewer What a Terrible Job Their Company, Program, or Department is Doing

I once had a client who, during an interview, rattled off a list of why the program they were interviewing to work for was so terrible and how they would change the entire program if they were hired. Needless to say, they did not make it to the next interview.

It's okay to want to help make a company or department run more efficiently (and the company would probably want that too!) but wait until you get the job and have had a chance to get a feel for the company or role before you try to suggest or implement sweeping changes.

Even if the company is openly stating that they are hiring someone to come in and fix internal issues, do not say negative things about the company, department, or their previous projects. They don't want to hire someone who is just going to bash the company. Instead, note some of the strengths you might have seen in the processes, employees, or projects, then follow that up with something like, "However, I would be excited to implement some ideas I have for improving [production, revenue, morale, organizational development, processes, etc.]." Be aware, though, that if you say something along these lines, then you had better have some actual ideas of how to do this and be willing to share at least one of those ideas with the interviewer.

Don't Wear Heavy Perfume or Cologne

While it's obviously good to smell nice for an interview, you don't want to overdo it. It's also important to note that some offices are scent-free so as to avoid aggravating employees' allergies.

Don't Be a Jackass (i.e., Don't Be Sexist, Racist, Homophobic, Classist, etc.)

This might seem like common sense… but you'd be surprised. Always be as polite as possible during an interview regardless of your opinion of the person interviewing you. I've had clients lose out on positions (rightly so!) because they complained (to the interviewer!) that the interview started late or that the company seemed unorganized. If something happens during the interview that makes you think less of the company, then keep it to yourself (unless it's something you can get clarification on during your questions at the end of the interview).

Interview Practice Questions

You may have heard of some companies asking totally off the wall questions like, "If you were a shape, what shape would you be?" or "What superhero would you be and why?" Most organizations realize they aren't going to get much information from those answers other than to get an idea of your personality. Instead, most companies typically opt for interview questions that will help them determine your previous experience and if that experience is the right fit for the role to which you're applying. In this section, we'll be focusing on the questions which most employers usually ask. We'll start with the question, explain what the employer is looking for, then provide a possible answer in italics.

Tell Me About Yourself

This is arguably one of the most widely used yet poorly answered questions during the interview. Almost every interviewer asks some variation of it as the very first question. The answer to this question sets the tone for the rest of the interview, yet most candidates don't bother to prep for it because how difficult can it be to talk about yourself? You know yourself better than anyone, right? Except, interviewers don't want to know everything about you. They want to know things about you that are related to the position for which you're interviewing.

Your answer to this question paints a picture of yourself to the interviewer. You want to make sure that picture shows a little of your personality while providing information about your background, relevant employment and/or education, and why you're excited about the position.

I've found that one of the best ways to answer this question and keep it relevant to the role is to instead think of it like the interviewer is asking, "What professional path brought you here today?" That makes it easier to craft an answer that tells a story that will keep the interviewer interested, as it will eventually relate back to what made you apply for the position with their company.

Be honest with your answers, but remember that whatever you say here is part of the interview. If you bring up something during your answer, that means that the interviewer can ask you about it. So, don't mention anything about a disability, your family, kids, religion, or politics.

Here are some examples to help you get an idea of how to create your own answer to the "tell me about yourself" question.

Example 1: Greg the prior military logistician interviewing for a Global Shipping Warehouse Manager role:

Tell me about yourself:

I'm originally from a small town in West Virginia and joined the Army so I could see more of the world as an Automated Logistics Technician. Over the course my eight years of service, I rose through the ranks to a Logistics Supervisor and eventually a Logistics Manager with 25 people under my direct supervision, a $2 million budget, and responsibility for over $5 million of equipment and supplies. I really enjoyed my time in service, but around 2012, I realized I was ready for a new challenge. I'd been picking up college courses here and there throughout my service but hadn't really had the chance to focus on school, so I decided to separate from the military in order to finish out my Bachelor's degree in Business Administration. With all the courses I'd completed while in the military, I only needed another two years of courses and I graduated in 2014; however, I found I really enjoyed school and wanted to learn more about applying business practices to the logistical chain lifecycle. I completed a Masters in Supply Chain Management, then had the opportunity to complete an internship with XYZ Inc. at their headquarters where I got to learn about all the moving parts of a global business. That experience is why I'm so excited to be interviewing for the Global Shipping Manager Warehouse position, as I would have the opportunity to blend my management skills from the military, my education, and my internship experience to further this organization's goals of fulfilling global requisitions.

Example 2: Carol the IT guru interviewing for a Help Desk Manager role

Tell me about yourself:

I've always been fascinated by technology. I was always the person my extended family would call when they had a computer or hardware issue, so you could say that I started as an unpaid IT help desk tech before I hit my teens. In college, I naturally pursued a degree in computer science and quickly completed the A+ CompTIA certification in my first year. While in school, I had the opportunity to work in the college's computer lab and provided in-person assistance to students struggling with computer, software, or hardware issues. My senior year I wanted to challenge myself a little more, so I took a work from home position as an IT Technician. I really enjoyed that and was able to assist the organization in identifying and migrating to a more effective trouble-ticket system, which earned me a promotion to IT Technician Supervisor. In my new role, I developed and implemented an online training program for over 200 remote technicians. Not long after that, I finished my degree and found that my position was no longer as challenging as it had been, which is why I'm so interested in this IT Technician Manager role as it appears that the organization is expanding its reach to cover more territory and will be bringing on more technicians. I think it would be an amazing opportunity to be a part of that expansion and play an integral role in on-boarding, training, and then managing the new technicians to provide the quality services that your organization is already known for.

Notice that both answers provide a larger, slightly more personal picture of the candidates, yet both stick to topics that are relevant to the position for which they are interviewing. Also, both end by providing a reason that the candidate is interested in the particular position to which they are applying. It's not just that they are interested in this industry, but they want to work in that particular role with that specific company.

The best method for preparing to answer this question is to write out your answer, then practice it until you have it memorized and it feels like a natural explanation.

What Is Your Greatest Strength/What Is Your Greatest Weakness?

While many hiring managers trying to fill higher-level positions have begun leaving these questions out, they are still something you should have an answer for. After all, as a professional, you should know what your greatest strength and your greatest weakness are.

And let's not give that bullshit answer of, "My greatest strength is also my greatest weakness—that I'm such a hard worker, blah, blah, blah." That answer is weak and by providing it, you've basically just wasted an opportunity to make yourself stand out from other candidates. Instead, let's explore how to provide strong, thought-provoking answers that make you stand out in the interviewer's mind in a positive way. First, let's tackle the easy one.

Greatest Strength

Don't tell the interviewer that your greatest strength is that you're a hard worker. After all, "hard worker" is a subjective phrase and will mean different things to different people. Do you mean you'll show up on time? Finish all projects well before deadline? Work late hours to get the job done? Provide support to your co-workers? If that's what you mean by hard worker, then say those things instead.

Better yet, let's construct an answer that puts you ahead of the other candidates. Your new answer is going to have two parts: what your greatest strength is and an example of that greatest strength in action from a previous job.

Before going any further, let's be clear that it's best to always be honest during interviews, otherwise you may get the job but you won't stay there very long once they detect any lies you told during the interview. Instead ask yourself what strengths you have that would be a great asset for the job. Read back through the job description to remind yourself what they are seeking. This should give you some ideas of what would be viewed as a great strength at this organization.

For example, say you're applying for a secretarial or administrative assistant position and the job description lists organizational skills as a qualification. If you have great organizational skills, then perhaps that's the best strength to list, but your answer shouldn't stop there.

The second part of answering this question is providing an example of your strength. This could be a specific example or it could be a general example.

Specific:

My greatest strength is an ability to organize even the craziest mess. In fact, my last supervisor recognized that I was good at organization and selected me above my peers to manage and organize the migration from paper documents to digital copies because he knew I wouldn't miss any documents and would finish before the deadline.

General:

My greatest strength is an ability to organize even the craziest mess. I was usually the person my supervisor assigned the more difficult organizational tasks to because he knew I had a knack for straightening out messes.

The main takeaway here is that your answer should be relevant to the position. You probably have a lot of strengths, but if it's not going to make you a stronger candidate for the position, then it doesn't make sense to provide that answer as a strength. Remember, too, that your greatest strength may not be something that you're good at doing, but rather something that you're passionate about, which has made you better at that thing.

Imagine someone interviewing for a tax accountant position who says:

My greatest strength is that I'm really fascinated by tax laws. I know that makes me sound like a giant nerd, but there's just something about understanding a new tax code and using it to save my clients money. My fascination with tax law and codes actually caught my last manager's attention and led to her assigning me as the lead tax accountant for a global corporation we'd just started working with. We didn't usually work with global accounts because of the global tax laws that might apply, but my boss knew I could handle learning all the required tax laws because it would be a new and fascinating thing to learn.

While the interviewer's first thought might be, "This guy is right! He is a geek!" Their next thought is probably going to be, "But he's clearly good at what he does if his manager gave him such a large account. Sounds like a good asset for our team."

Greatest Weakness

On the flip side of the coin, you must answer what your greatest weakness is. As previously mentioned, it is not a good idea to try and convince the interviewer that your biggest weakness is that you work too hard. This answer is old and tired. Everyone who thinks they are clever tries to use this as an answer, but all it does is make the interviewer want to roll their eyes.

Instead give a real answer to this question. I know it might seem unnerving to reveal a true weakness, but doing so will make you stand out to a hiring manager. Also, because you're going to always provide a two-part answer to this question, the second part of your answer will demonstrate your professionalism.

Let's focus on the first part of your answer: the actual weakness. Ask yourself what your actual weaknesses in the workplace are. Are you unorganized? Are you less than great at returning emails or phone calls? Do you tend to get too caught up in perfection and not finish projects on time? While being honest with your answer is good, you'll still want to avoid telling an employer a weakness that might be detrimental to you performing well in the position. In other words, you wouldn't interview for an IT Customer Service/Help Desk position and tell the hiring manager that you're terrible at communicating with customers. That's a weakness that, if revealed, would keep you from getting the job.

Try to focus on a weakness that won't be integral to the position. To follow through on the above example of interviewing for the IT Customer Service/Help Desk position, you might instead say something like:

My greatest weakness is that I sometimes spend too long assisting customers. I'm quick in identifying and remedying their initial IT problem but then I make the mistake of asking if they need anything else and get caught up in trying to solve other IT issues or questions they have that aren't related to the initial trouble-ticket.

This answer rings of truth and seems to reveal an actual weakness this applicant has discovered about themselves. It's an actual problem since there are probably other customers waiting for the IT Technician to call them and fix their technical issues. If the applicant just left their answer at that, then it could potentially hurt them. Sure, they were honest about their weakness, but this weakness could be an issue on the job.

However, remember that you're always going to give two answers to this question. The first is what the weakness is and the second part is how you've started working on fixing that weakness. After all, if you're truly a professional, then when you notice you have a weakness that might affect your work, you should take steps to address that weakness. This is what employers actually care about when they ask you about your greatest weakness.

Using the above weakness example, the applicant should then explain what steps they've taken to fix that weakness. It might sound something like this:

At my last position, when I noticed I was taking longer than I should to end service calls with customers after I'd already resolved their technical issue, I decided to implement a five-minute rule for myself. I still wanted to provide a positive experience for customers and felt the need to ask them if they needed anything else after I'd resolved their computer problem, but once I solved the initial problem, I'd start a timer and give myself only another five minutes to wrap up the call with them. This really worked and has helped me move on to the next customer waiting for assistance without losing that quality connection with the first customer.

This answer is going to impress the hiring manager because 1) the applicant came up with a solution to their problem and 2) it not only improved their ability to assist more clients in a day, the applicant is also showing that they care about the customer service experience and wanted to make sure that it didn't suffer.

To sum up, make sure whatever weakness answer you decide to provide is 1) true, 2) not going to ruin your chances for the job, and 3) includes how you're working to improve it.

Situational Questions & The STAR Method

If you've sat for any kind of interviews, you'll be familiar with the following kind of questions even if you don't know what they are called. Situational questions typically start with, "Tell me about a time when…" then continue by asking for a specific example of a time you experienced something or did something at work, and most importantly, how you handled it. That last piece is the clincher and is what the hiring manager actually wants to hear about.

These questions can feel a little intimidating because the answers can easily go off the rails, especially while explaining the situation to set up your answer. But if you train yourself to use a technique called the STAR method, you'll find it's a little easier to formulate your answers concisely.

STAR Method

The STAR method is simply a process for organizing your answers to situational interview questions. The letters are an acronym and stand for four parts of an interview answer: Situation, Task, Action, and Result.

Situation

During situational interview questions, the interviewers are asking for a specific example from your previous positions or volunteer experiences. In the first part of your answer, you're merely setting up the context of your answer for the interviewer so that they'll have a clear understanding of the circumstances surrounding your answer. Try to keep the Situation portion of your answer short and concise, as you don't want to run the risk of losing the interviewer's attention or interest.

Situation Example:

While I was working for XYZ Inc. as a Sales Representative, I found that I was really struggling to communicate clearly with my supervisor as I only ever saw her at bi-monthly meetings. Unfortunately, the poor communication between us was beginning to affect both me and my team's productivity as we would sometimes not find out about new sales initiatives until the bi-monthly meetings.

Task

The next step of answering the situational question is to explain what your specific task was. Sometimes this will be a task that was appointed to you by a supervisor and other times it will be a self-appointed task for when you tried to solve a problem.

Task Example:

While most of my colleagues felt the problem would eventually work itself out when we would inevitably lose sales due to lack of communication, I felt that it was our responsibility to speak up before that happened and let our manager know that there was a problem.

Action

In the next section of your answer, you're going to explain what Action you took in this situation. This is the part that the interviewers are looking for. Remember, interviewers are asking you situational questions to see how you respond in certain situations, that way they can try to gauge how well you'd do as an employee at their company.

The below example might seem lengthy, but it's important to lay out details to the interviewer about how you navigated the problem.

Action Example:

I called our manager and asked if she had time to speak one-on-one with me outside of the bi-monthly meeting at a later date. I made sure she understood that while the meeting was important to me, it wasn't about anything bad. I didn't want her to think I was quitting! We set up an in-person meeting during which I was able to explain the communication issues that the sales department was experiencing. I laid out some of the specific contract losses we'd experienced due to lack of communication, but I was careful not to place any blame on anyone. I also offered some suggestions on alternative methods we might try in order to improve our communication with her, such as meeting weekly or supplementing bi-monthly meetings with a weekly email about any major sales opportunities, new internal initiatives, or contract opportunities.

Result

For the last portion of your answer, you'll explain what the results of your actions were. It's important to note that you should try to use situations for your situational answers that had at least moderately positive outcomes. You don't want to lay out an entire answer only to have the result be that you were ultimately fired or quit the job because the problem couldn't be resolved! If that's true of a situation, then pick a situation with a happier ending.

Result Example:

My manager ultimately ended up thanking me for bringing the issue to her attention. She explained first to me, and then to the entire sales team during our next meeting, that she'd simply stuck with the bi-monthly sales meetings since they were already in place when she'd taken the job not long ago and since none of the sales team had mentioned anything, she hadn't thought there was a problem. However, she had noticed that sales numbers were slipping, but had been attributing those losses to other factors. She ended up offering the team the options I'd suggested and allowed us to select what we thought would work best, with the promise that we'd reevaluate how communication was working in three months after implementing one of the solutions. After implementing a weekly email to supplement the bi-monthly meetings, our communication vastly improved and sales numbers actually increased by 15%!

If you use the STAR method to organize your answers to situational questions into blocks that address the Situation, your specific Task, what Actions you took, and what the Results of your actions were, you'll be less likely to be side-tracked by irrelevant details and more likely to fully answer the question in a way that paints a positive picture of your abilities to the interviewer.

Interview Questions to Prepare For

While you can't intuit all the situational questions an interviewer might ask, there are a few that it's good to already have an answer for. Many of your answers to the following situational questions can be altered as needed to fit other questions should you be asked something slightly different. Rather than provide you with suggested answers, instead, I'm going to tell you what the interviewer is usually looking for in the answer.

Tell me about a time you disagreed with your supervisor

What employers really want to know here is how you handled or resolved the situation. After all, they want an employee who will act like an adult during disagreements or conflicts. Most employers are usually looking for an answer that involves the employee speaking to their supervisor first to see if they can work out the issue. If the issue is something that continued even after addressing it with a supervisor, then the employer wants to know that you won't just quit the job. Instead, they want to know if you utilized the appropriate chain of command and raised the issue to the supervisor's manager for discussion.

Tell me about a time you didn't get along with a co-worker

Similar to the previous question, employers want to know that you're able to handle such a situation with maturity. They want to hear about how you tried to resolve the issue at the lowest level by speaking directly with that co-worker. If the issue wasn't resolved and it continued to affect your work, they then want to hear how you approached your supervisor to discuss the issue.

If you're applying for a position that involves customer service, be prepared to answer a question like, "Tell me about a time you had to deal with a difficult customer." If you are applying to be a supervisor or manager, you might field a question like, "Tell me about a time you had to deal with a difficult employee."

Note: For both of the above questions, it's good to try to come up with examples that had a positive resolution. If you bring up an example that made you quit the job, then it's probably not the best example to give. You don't want an employer to think you'll simply quit when faced with a difficult problem.

Tell me about an especially difficult project or assignment you've had

Here the employer doesn't actually care about what the project was, but rather how you tend to respond during difficulties. They want to hear about your innovation in coming up with solutions, your ability to work under pressure, and that you didn't immediately run to your supervisor when you ran into issues.

The answer to this question can be used for a number of other situational questions revolving around difficult projects or projects that you're proud of.

Tell me about a time you failed

Don't tell the interviewer that you've never failed. They'll call bullshit and wonder about the veracity of your other interview answers. Everyone has failed at something in their life at some point. The employer doesn't care that you failed. Rather, they want to know how you handled that failure and more importantly, what you learned from it.

Other ways you may hear this question are:

"Tell me about a time you weren't able to complete an assignment."

"Tell me about time that a client was unhappy with your work."

Tell me about a time you had to manage/handle a heavy workload

In this situational question, the employer is seeing how you juggle priorities and handle stress at work. Make sure your answer includes how you prioritized your assignments before tackling them.

Tell me about a time you had to deal with an ethical dilemma at work

This one can feel tricky, but really employers want to make sure that you are an ethical employee and that you can follow the organization's policy on how to handle such situations at work.

You might have to really mull this one over before you're able to come up with a good example. Try to give an answer that paints you in a positive light. You don't want to tell an employer that you knew that someone at work was being unethical but you decided to just not tell anyone.

Next-Level Interviewing: Practice, Practice, Practice

Take your interview preparation to the next level by heavily reviewing the job description before the interview. Review every duty, experience, and skill listed in the job description and turn it into a question that you must answer with a specific example of your experience. Use the above STAR method to answer these job description questions with specific situations from your work experience.

Example 1:

> Job Description: Candidates must have experience with providing excellent customer service.
>
> Practice Question: Tell me about your experience in providing excellent customer service and give me an example.

Example 2:

> Job Description: Strong applicants much have experience maintaining files in a database.
>
> Practice Question: Tell me about your experience maintaining files using an electronic database and give me an example of a time you went above and beyond in managing/maintaining files.

Example 3:

> Job Description: Strong candidates will be able to work independently with little supervision.
>
> Practice Question: Tell me about a time/position in which you worked independently with little to no supervision.

Preparing for an interview by ensuring you have an answer ready for every duty or responsibility listed in the job description will ensure that you have a specific situation ready in the back of your mind for whatever the interviewer might ask. It will also boost your confidence before the interview since you'll know you meet all of the requirements for the position (and have examples to back up just how well-qualified you are!)

Questions to Ask the Interviewer

Always keep in mind that an interview is not just about the employer making sure you're a good fit for the role. It's also your opportunity to make sure the role is a good fit for you. An interview gives you the chance to make sure that you would enjoy the job, get along with the people you'd work with, and like the company and the company culture.

While you can sometimes get hints during the interview about what a company or position might be like, the best time to find out more about your fit with the company and/or the role is when the interviewer asks you if you have any questions.

The answer to this question is ALWAYS yes.

Not having questions for the interviewer is the kiss of death in most interviews. If you say that you don't have any questions, you're indicating to the employer that you're really not interested in the role. But you wouldn't be interviewing if you weren't interested, right? So show the employer you really want the job by asking intelligent questions that give you a better glimpse into the role, the company, and the company culture.

Stay away from asking about benefits and salary. I know it's an important factor, but it's not really a conversation to have until you have an official offer.

Instead, before the interview, go ahead and come up with four to five questions to ask. It's good to have that many questions ready because some of them may get answered in the natural course of your conversation during the interview. You can write these questions down in your notepad and bring them to the interview so you remember what they are.

For some ideas of questions to ask, check out the list of potential questions below. Consider trying a mix of questions that allow you to learn more about the different aspects of the role. Just make sure to double check the job description to make sure that the information within doesn't already answer any of your questions!

Questions About the Position

What accomplishments would be expected of me in the role at 30, 60, and 90 days?

I like this question because it allows you to get a better idea of what expectations the employer has if you were to be given the position. Sometimes this can help you weed out a position that has unrealistic expectations for its employees or help you determine if a role would not be challenging enough to keep your attention.

Alternatively, you can cut this question down to merely ask what would be expected of you within the first 90 days in the role.

What skills and experience do you feel would make an ideal candidate for this role besides those in the job description?

This is a great open-ended question that will have the interviewer put his or her cards on the table and state exactly what the employer is looking for. If the interviewer mentions something you didn't cover yet, now is your chance to bring up that skill!

However, I have also seen some interviewers give unhelpful answers in which they merely state that they are looking for someone who matches the job description. Since you'll most likely be asking these questions at the end of the interview, you'll need to gauge whether or not this question will be beneficial to ask that particular interviewer.

What was the single largest challenge faced by employees in this position in the past?

I find this question useful for several reasons. First, it will give you a better idea of what your biggest challenge would be were you to accept the role. If the interviewer relays a challenge that you've breezed through in the past, then this may be a good position for you. However, if the challenge faced by those in this role is something that you've struggled with in the past (or maybe you quit your last job over a similar issue), then you'll be better able to determine if you really want to take the job and potentially face the challenge again.

Second, the question can potentially help you discover if there have been issues with retaining people in this role (depending on how much information the interviewer lets slip).

If you've already learned that this is a totally new role, then you might tweak this question to ask what challenges you might expect to face were you to be offered the role.

What constitutes success in this position OR in this department, firm, or nonprofit?

This question shows your interest in being successful there. Plus, the answer will show you how to get ahead and whether the role would be a good fit for you.

Do you have any hesitations about my qualifications? (OR) Now that we've talked about my qualifications and the job, do you have any concerns about my being successful in this position?

I love this question because it's gutsy. It demonstrates that you're confident in your skills and abilities. But it also allows the interviewer to address any concerns they might have regarding a skill you didn't mention during the interview or something you said during your previous answers. I've had a client who salvaged a crumbling interview with this question since it gave them the chance to address the interviewer's concern that the client hadn't mentioned a specific skill (that the client did possess).

However, if you already know that you have a gap in skills/experience for this position, perhaps avoid asking this question since it will only remind the interviewer that you lack a certain skill.

Can you tell me about the team I'd be working with?

This question is useful for gauging what to expect regarding your co-workers, supervisor, and/or manager. It can help you determine how many co-workers you would have, if they'd be in the same office, or if you'd be the only one performing this role.

Questions About the Organization/Company

Do you offer continuing education and professional training?

This question shows that you're interested in continued professional development, which most companies appreciate in an employee.

What can you tell me about the company's new products or plans for growth?

This question should be customized for your particular needs. Do your homework on the employer's website beforehand and mention a new product or service it's launching to demonstrate your research and interest. The answer to this question will give you a good idea of where the company is headed.

Questions About the Interviewer

What have you enjoyed most about working here?

This question allows the interviewer to connect with you on a more personal level by sharing his or her feelings. The answer will also give you unique insight into how satisfied people are with their jobs there. If the interviewer looks pained when coming up with an answer to your question, it's a big red flag.

How long have you been with the company? (AND/OR) Did you start out at this company in your current role?

I find this useful for determining if the company retains its good employees or if the place is a revolving door of unhappy personnel.

Last But Not Least

What is the next step in the process?

This is essentially the last question and one you should definitely ask. It shows that you're interested in moving forward in the process and invites the interviewer to tell you how many people are in the running for the position. You may also get more information about when you'll hear back from the interviewer about whether you've been selected or not.

Chapter 8
Salary Negotiation

If you're concerned about negotiating your salary, you're not alone. Almost every client I've worked with has expressed concerns about salary negotiation. Whether it's trying to figure out exactly how much to ask for or how to go about submitting a counteroffer, negotiating your salary after receiving an offer can feel daunting to say the least.

However, by following these next suggestions, you'll be more likely to succeed in nailing down a salary that aligns with your experience, skills, and education.

Setting Realistic Expectations

Having unrealistic expectations about what you deserve to be paid for a role can hurt you in one of two ways: 1) Setting your salary expectations too high will keep you from accepting positions with pay that you feel is too low and 2) Setting your salary expectations too low will keep you in a perpetual state of taking roles for which you are underpaid.

It's important to find that happy middle ground and identify what would be a realistic salary range that accurately represents your experience and that you would be willing to accept.

I've found that the two main things that hold people back from identifying a realistic salary range are:

1) Viewing their salary as a direct reflection of their own self-worth
2) Expecting a certain salary because they want to maintain an expensive lifestyle

Let's look at each one of these issues individually.

Salary and Self-Worth

It's unfortunate but true that our society tends to put a lot of emphasis on the importance of money and generally smiles upon those people who make a lot of it. No wonder our sense of self-esteem can be directly affected by how much we make in a position. This feeling of inadequacy can become even more prevalent when our friends and/or family have positions with high salaries. Because of this, it's difficult to separate our feelings of self-worth from the amount in our paychecks. However, the reality is that we are getting paid for the skills, education, and experience that we possess. It's also important to remember that our society holds some positions in higher esteem (sometimes seemingly arbitrarily) and rewards those roles with higher rates of pay.

The reverse of this issue is also true. Some people feel that they shouldn't be paid a high salary for their position and so perpetually stay in low-paying roles. This is usually seen within human services industries such as social work or mental health counseling and is most prevalent among those in the nonprofit sector. The unfortunate and false idea here is that in order to work within the human services industry or make a difference in your community, you have to be selfless and therefore only accept low-paying positions. Accepting a role that pays a higher amount is seen by many in this industry as being greedy. This way of thinking tends to keep those in the human services industry from accepting higher salaries that are more in line with their experience and education.

Maintaining an Expensive Lifestyle

The second issue that tends to hold applicants back from identifying a realistic salary is that they are attempting to maintain an expensive lifestyle and so only consider positions with a high rate of pay. Of course, this is only an issue if their experience, skills, and education don't align with that salary range. If they've already made that amount previously and are staying in the same industry, then their expectations are likely realistic.

However, if they've previously made that amount but they're switching to an entirely different industry, then it's likely that they'll need to adjust their salary expectations to be more in line with the salary ranges for that new industry.

This is also true of someone just starting out in a new field. If an applicant has little to no experience in an industry or position, then they should expect to start out on the lower end of a salary range. Just because an applicant needs to make a certain amount in order to maintain their current lifestyle, doesn't actually mean that their skills and experience are worth that salary.

How to Identify a Realistic Salary Range

In order to identify a realistic salary range, the first thing you have to do is try and distance yourself from the emotional aspects of a salary. Instead, focus on the facts and identify your experience, education, and skills that are relevant to the positions to which you're applying.

Next, you'll need to do a little research. A great place to start is with O*Net's online database (www.onetonline.org) which is sponsored by the U.S. Department of Labor. Using this free database, you can research general fields of work and get information regarding the national and state average salaries for that field. The site also provides information regarding the estimated salary range and what are considered to be the "low," "average," and "high" salaries for that field.

I've found that this is a great way to get a baseline idea for what salary you should be looking for in a role. If you're just starting out in a field, then you should expect to land on the low to average end of that salary range. If you've been in that field for several years, then you should expect to land on the average to high end of the salary range. Other factors that can affect where you land on the salary range are your education and training relevant to that field. If you possess specific degrees or certifications that are not required but highly respected in that field, then that may push you up to a higher salary.

Remember that this is just a baseline to give you a ballpark salary range.

To get a better idea of what salary you can expect for a particular role with a specific company, you'll need to do more research using websites like Glassdoor, Payscale, Salary, or Indeed. Though most of these sites are a paid service, you can usually get several searches for free before they require you to sign up and pay for their services. Using these sites might provide a glimpse into what you can expect for a salary in specific positions. Just keep in mind that the numbers generated are usually based off of what the previous person employed in that role received and might be a slightly higher or lower amount than what you would receive.

You'll be taking the majority of your research, especially the information you learned from O*Net, and applying it during the actual negotiation.

How to Actually Negotiate

The main thing to always keep in mind when negotiating a salary (or a raise) is that the conversation is not about what you need financially. Even if that's the underlying reason that you're trying to gain a higher offer, that should not be the focal point of your argument. Instead, you are negotiating a higher salary because your education, skills, and experience make you deserving of a higher salary. Basically speaking, you should get paid what you're worth.

However, when determining what to expect in a salary, other factors actually surpass the importance of what your experience is worth. Factors such as what the employer is willing to pay and the national or state average salary for that position take precedence over your experience. Take a look at the graphic below to gain a better understanding of what factors you should keep in mind when determining what salary to expect.

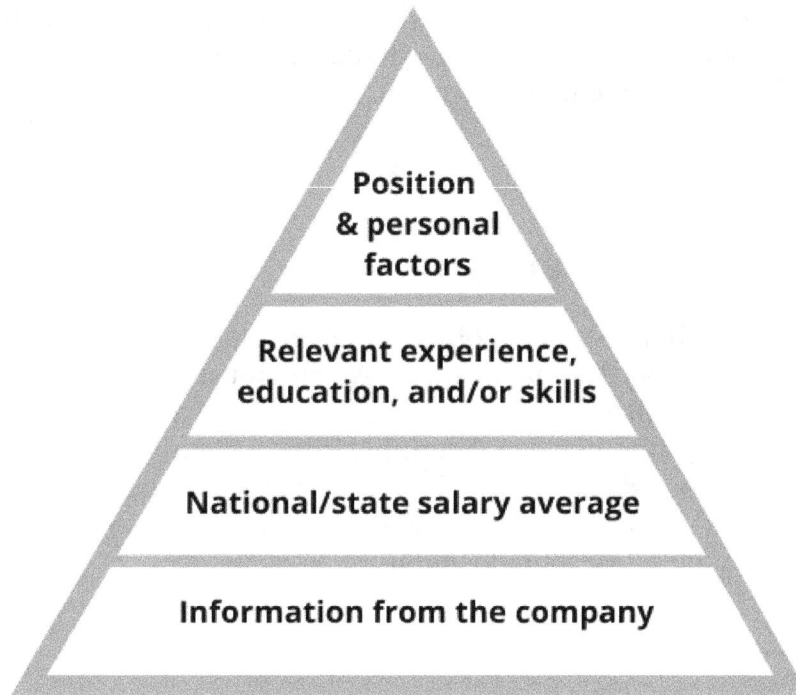

Salary Negotiation Factors

Information from the Company

As you can see from the above figure, the first item that determines the salary you should expect comes from the base of the pyramid and should act as the foundation of what leads to the amount you ask for. That foundation consists of any salary information you've gained from the employer. Whether listed in the job description or explained during an interview, if you've received information from the employer regarding what salary range to expect from a position, then that should be the main factor you consider when determining what salary to expect.

If an employer explicitly states in writing or during an interview what the salary range is for a role, then it's not wise to expect a higher amount than that. Unless you have some insider information from someone working within that organization who has told you that the company is willing to pay more, then expect your salary to fall within the stated range. Seeking a higher salary than what was discussed or stated on the job description will usually only prove a useless endeavor. This is especially true if you're not even open to accepting the position at the highest end of the range. An employer is likely to view willfully ignoring the stated salary range as an annoyance and might not be open to considering you for future roles.

That said, there are occasionally factors that might prompt the company to offer an amount at a rate higher than the stated salary range. Such factors might include an initial relocation reimbursement or if the position is in a location with a higher cost of living that wasn't figured into the initially stated salary range. However, being offered a position with a salary that is higher than the listed salary range is the exception, not the norm.

National or State Salary Averages

The next thing that will help you negotiate a higher salary is to do some research regarding the national or state average salary for that position. As previously mentioned, you can find this data on O*Net's free online database.

When receiving a job offer, you can determine if the offered salary is below or above average for that position in your specific state. Knowing these averages will help you decide if the employer is low-balling you on their offer or if the amount they're offering is within an acceptable range for the position and your geographic location.

Relevant Experience, Education, and/or Skills

Many applicants make the mistake of thinking that these are the only factors that determine one's salary. While your education and experience are important, employers determine compensation for positions based on what they've paid in the past for that position and on what the average compensation is for that kind of role. A candidate's experience, education, and skills only come into play after those first two factors are determined.

This is why it's so important to know exactly what skills, education, and experience you possess that are important to the employer for this particular position. If you've made it through the interview process and have received a job offer, then hopefully you'll know at this point just what experience and/or skills the employer finds important. These factors will be used to determine where your salary will fall within the employer's predetermined compensation range.

If your experience or education surpasses the basic position requirements, then you'll likely be offered an amount on the higher end of the salary range. If an employer doesn't think they have to spend extra time training you in the role or you've already shown in past positions that you excel in such a role, then the employer will want to lock in your talent, likely offering you an amount on the high end of the range.

However, if your experience, skills, or education only meet the basic requirements of the position, then expect to receive an offer on the mid-to-lower end of that range.

Position and Personal Factors

Lastly, a factor that you'll want to take into account when negotiating your salary is what the requirements or major responsibilities of the position are. Hopefully the job description is quite clear about your expected responsibilities in the position, but occasionally, you may encounter a position that turns out to require different responsibilities than those listed in the job description.

For example, I once interviewed for a position that seemed fairly straightforward in the job description, but during the interview, I learned that the role was a first of its kind and I would therefore be implementing a completely new program that would require extensive travel and project management. None of this was mentioned in the job description or in the initial interview. Only in the second interview when I asked more probing questions about the expectations of the role did I gain a better understanding of the position's daily responsibilities. Had I not asked questions and learned about the actual expectations of the role, I would have accepted the initial salary offer since it was in line with my original understanding of the position's expectations. However, armed with the new information about what I would actually be expected to accomplish in the position, I asked for at least $10,000 more for my salary.

Besides the position's expected responsibilities, another factor to consider when determining salary includes identifying if it's a dangerous role. Maybe it has you climbing tall structures, handling potentially dangerous equipment, or controlling deadly materials. If these factors are already figured into the salary, then you'll be paid at a slightly higher rate than someone who does a similar job without the same level of danger.

Lastly, when negotiating a higher salary, you'll want to consider personal factors. The main example of this would be if you already have health insurance and don't need to be covered by the employer. This means the employer is potentially saving around $1500 to $3000 a year by not paying to provide you with health insurance. You may try to negotiate a higher salary since by hiring you, they'd be saving money.

Putting it All Together into an Effective Argument

Once you have a grasp of the above four factors, you'll be able to create a more cohesive argument as to why you deserve to start the role at a higher amount. Remember, it's not about why you *need* a higher salary, but why you *deserve* a higher salary. If a company wishes to gain the benefits of your experience and have you put that experience to work for them, then they should provide you with a salary that aligns with what they are gaining.

Here are some examples for how you might word a negotiation when asking for a higher salary based on the different factors above.

Salary Range Factor Example:

I'm excited about the prospect of working for XYZ Inc., but the offered salary of $32,000 is quite a bit lower than the initial salary range of $35,000 - $42,000 that was originally listed in the job description. With my recent internship in this field, I do feel that a starting range of $36,000 would be more in line with my experience and education.

Average Salary & Experience Factor Example:

I really appreciate the offer and hope to accept the role; however, my research shows that $47,000 is actually $5,000 lower than the average salary for similar positions in this region. As a mid-career employee in this industry, I feel that my experience would be more in line with an amount that is slightly above the average salary for this role, which is why I'm asking for $55,000 instead.

Experience, Skills, and/or Education Factor Example:

While I'm very excited to accept this position, I do wish to negotiate a salary higher than $67,000 that would be more in line with my 12 years of experience and advanced level of education. I feel that with my direct experience managing major projects while supervising a large group of personnel, I'll be able to successfully complete XYZ Inc.'s global projects while staying well below budget, bolstering employee morale, and increasing employees' productivity. Keeping this experience in mind, I feel that $72,000 would be a more appropriate starting salary.

Position and Personal Factors Example:

I am very excited about the prospect of starting with XYZ Inc. as a Senior Technician; however, I do wish to negotiate a higher starting salary. During the course of the interview, I was interested to learn that the Senior Technician is actually a new role and will be spearheading the creation of a new department including the hiring and training of a 40-person crew. While I'm enthusiastic about getting started on these projects, I do feel that the responsibility of hiring and training an entire department warrants a higher starting wage. As such, I feel that $50,000 is much more in line with the role's responsibilities.

Again, remember that asking for a higher salary is about why you deserve to be paid more. Keep your request short and stay on point about why you deserve a higher salary.

Counteroffer

When you decide to ask for a higher salary than the one initially offered by the employer, you're initiating a counteroffer. That is, you're saying that you're interested in the position, but you feel that you deserve a higher amount and you're telling the employer what that amount is.

However, it's very important to keep in mind that when you initiate a counteroffer, you are technically taking the original offer off the table. This means that there is a possibility that the employer could tell you that they are no longer interested in you as a candidate. Though it rarely occurs that an employer completely rescinds their job offer, you should know that it does occasionally happen.

It is much more likely that an employer will respond to your counteroffer in one of three ways:

1) They'll accept your counteroffer and start you at the requested higher salary.
2) They'll respond with a new number that is higher than your original offer but lower than the amount you requested.
3) They'll respond that the salary is fixed and you can take it or leave it.

Obviously, that first option is the one you're shooting for, but the second option is also beneficial as it still gives you a higher pay rate than the original offer.

Before you make a counteroffer, it's smart to determine what is the lowest amount for which you'd be willing to accept the role. Then, when submitting a counteroffer, ask for a salary that is at least a little higher than the lowest amount you'll accept. That way, if the employer responds with an amount that is between your requested salary and the amount originally offered, you'll be more likely to still be above your lowest acceptable salary rate.

Closing

Above all the previous recommendations and suggestions in this book, remember that landing a great, well-paid position takes patience and persistence. You may find that in order to land your dream role or gain access to the company you really want to work for, you have to take an interim role where you can gain more hands-on experience or make the right connections.

Just keep your resume updated and your LinkedIn profile polished in case the right position comes along. Then you'll be ready to put yourself forward as a professional, well-qualified candidate who wows the hiring manager.

Resources

The following resources are included to assist you in your job search and application efforts. Though these resources might be helpful, keep in mind that there are a myriad of other online and local resources available to you.

Job Search Resources

Recruiters

- Randstad – Frequently has positions in many fields and at all levels within the manufacturing and production industry.

  *Veteran Friendly; www.Randstad.com

- People Scout – Represent positions across almost all industries.

  *Veteran Friendly; www.PeopleScout.com

- AeroTek – Originally represented positions in aerospace and defense; now represent a multitude of industries at all levels.

  *Veteran Friendly; www.AeroTek.com

- RobertHalf – Primarily has professional office-related roles at all levels.

  www.roberthalf.com

Job Search Websites

- Indeed.com (general job search)
- ZipRecruiter (general job search)
- Dice.com (roles in information technology and related fields)
- USAJobs.org (federal job search—you need a federal resume to apply for these roles)

Employment Assistance

Career One Stop

Find a local American Job Center for assistance: https://www.careeronestop.org/Site/american-job-center.aspx

Wounded Warrior Project

Employment assistance in the form of job search coaching, resume assistance, and interview preparation. For veterans and their caregivers. www.woundedwarriorproject.org

Hire Heroes USA

Employment assistance in the form of resume assistance and interview preparation. For veterans and military spouses. https://www.hireheroesusa.org/

Interview Practice Resources

- Easy Hire – Provides one free interview session
  https://easyhire.me
- Assessment Day – Provides free interview video practice without feedback
  https://www.assessmentday.co.uk/video-interviews.htm
- Interview Buddy – Not free; provides interview feedback
  https://www.interviewbuddy.in/#Pricing

Interview Attire Assistance

Dress for Success

Provides professional attire and development tools to women. https://dressforsuccess.org/client-services/

Career Gear

Provides professional attire and development tools to youth (16-24), veterans, or those re-entering the workforce after incarceration or who are entering a 2nd or 3rd career. https://www.careergear.org/

Action Verbs for Resume

Supervised	Managed	Directed	Handled
Assessed	Analyzed	Researched	Troubleshot
Diagnosed	Produced	Created	Developed
Implemented	Updated	Provided	Answered
Administered	Monitored	Maintained	Received
Distributed	Sorted	Evaluated	Inventoried
Authored	Wrote	Budgeted	Mentored
Reviewed	Advised	Recommended	Suggested
Completed	Processed	Facilitated	Coordinated
Collaborated	Conducted	Assisted	Participated
Strengthened	Improved	Initiated	Lowered
Reduced	Awarded	Increased	Redesigned
Planned	Strategized	Recovered	Earned
Controlled	Observed	Communicated	Transmitted
Compiled	Served	Serviced	Outsourced
Delivered	Customized	Captured	Ascertained

Cover Letter Examples

The following cover letter templates are yours to do with what you will. Use them word for word (using your personal information of course and inserting the appropriate company and job title) or just use them piecemeal as needed. Whatever works for you!

Your Name
Street Address
City, State Zip
555-555-5555
YourEmail@email.com

Date Sending (January 6, 2020 format)

Re: Emergency Response Manager

Dear Mr. Anderson,

I was excited to learn of the Emergency Response Manager role with the city of Benton and am very interested in applying for the position as I will be relocating to the region next month.

I feel that I would be a great fit for this position as I have over 6 years of experience assessing, developing, and implementing emergency response plans for a municipal entity. During my time as a Safety & Risk Mitigation Manager for Ellicott City, I updated the city's emergency management plans in order to ensure readiness for any potential threats or natural disasters. I also took the opportunity to create back-up response plans in case of technological failure which proved useful during Hurricane Sandy as it allowed the city to still operate at 45% capabilities rather than zero.

Another reason I feel that I am a great candidate for this role is that I have ample experience in training government and civilian personnel in appropriate emergency response actions and regularly facilitated a variety of drills to ensure true readiness. I also incorporated online learning technologies in order to provide bi-annual preparedness trainings to supplement live response drills. With this experience, I feel that I would be able to ensure that 100% of your staff would be ready to respond to any natural or man-made threats in the workplace.

Lastly, I am truly passionate about providing a safe environment for our government employees. Though I'm well-versed in safety codes and regulations, emergency management isn't just about being up to code on paper. It's also about ensuring all employees feel safe in their work environment and know immediately what to do in case of an emergency.

With my passion for ensuring staff safety coupled with my experience in evaluating and training personnel in emergency management response, I truly feel that I am the ideal candidate for the Emergency Response Manager role.

I look forward to hearing from you.

Sincerely,

Your Name

Cover Letter 1: Moving

Your Name
Street Address
City, State Zip
555-555-5555
YourEmail@email.com

Date Sending (January 6, 2020 format)

Re: Tax Accountant

Dear Mrs. Smith,

I was excited to learn of the Tax Accountant role from a previous co-worker, John Doe, who is now the Accounting Manager over that position, and am very interested in applying for the role.

I feel that I would be a great fit for the position as, during my 4 years as a Tax Accountant for Big Little Accounts, I managed to gain the organization 12 major global accounts through organic outreach and satisfied customer referrals which led to an increase in the organization's overall revenue by 24%. Year over year, I also managed to retain 100% of my accounts by providing a quality customer service experience during every interaction.

Another reason I feel that I am a great candidate for this role is that I find it very important to always continue learning and growing within my field and, as such, I am constantly learning tax laws which open new opportunities for clients with a variety of tax requests. While working as a Tax Specialist for Russell Tax Services, I became proficient in international tax law and was then able to take on global accounts not previously serviced by the organization.

Lastly, I am truly fascinated by tax laws and passionate about providing a great customer service experience to all clients regardless of company size. With my 10 years of Tax Accounting experience, my ability to build a robust client portfolio, and my passion for ensuring customer satisfaction and retention, I truly feel that I am the ideal candidate for the Tax Accountant position and would greatly benefit your organization's bottom line.

I look forward to hearing from you.

Sincerely,

Your Name

Cover Letter 2: Name Drop

Your Name
Street Address
City, State Zip
555-555-5555
YourEmail@email.com

Date Sending (January 6, 2020 format)

Re: Virtual Customer Service Representative

Dear Mr. Smith,

I was excited to learn of the Virtual Customer Service Representative role with Virtual Services Now and am very interested in applying for the position.

I feel that I would be a great fit for this home-based position as I'm a customer service specialist who thrives in a home-based work environment. During my 3 years as a Customer Service Assistant for Data Cell Inc., I worked remotely from my home office and gained extensive experience in independently prioritizing, organizing, and completing tasks within assigned timelines. As such, I was selected above 25 peers to mentor and train other home-based personnel in the best practices for working from home.

Another reason I feel that I am a great candidate for this role is that I truly want to ensure that customers receive a positive experience during all interactions. My experience at both Data Cell Inc. and at T Mobile as an Account Representative taught me that the first step to problem resolution is simply making sure the customer knows they've been heard. This method allowed me to make a positive impact on over 245 customers at T Mobile who left me a 5-star customer service review and also led to a 34% bump in customer retention.

Lastly, I am a big believer that customers should not be able to tell that their customer service representative is working from home. I ensure that customer service calls remain professional by maintaining a separate, noise-free home office space with a high-speed internet connection.

With my passion for providing 5-star customer service and my ability to work independently coupled with my dedication to maintaining a noise-free home office environment for professional calls, I feel that I am truly a great candidate for the Virtual Customer Service Representative position at Virtual Services Now.

I look forward to hearing from you.

Sincerely,

Your Name

Cover Letter 3: Work from Home

Your Name
Street Address
City, State Zip
555-555-5555
YourEmail@email.com

Date Sending (January 6, 2020 format)

Re: Intelligence Manager

Dear Mrs. Smith,

I was excited to learn of the Intelligence Manager role with VK Contract Services and am writing to inform you of my intention to apply for the position.

I feel that I would be a great fit for the position as I gained extensive experience in the collection, analysis, and appropriate dissemination of intelligence during my 15 years as a Military Intelligence Manager in the U.S. Army. During my service, I regularly managed multiple intelligence projects across several regions simultaneously with cross-functional teams consisting of 5-25 personnel. I would be excited to apply this experience to the Intelligence Manager role with VK Contract Services and feel I would help the organization to gain even more Department of Defense contracts by leading the intelligence team to achieve great success and exceed contractual expectations.

Another reason I would be a great candidate for the role is that I was regularly commended for my ability to develop successful intelligence collection training programs for both military and civilian contractor partners. In 2017, I was selected above my peers to assess and update the existing program delivered to military personnel who were training to become intelligence analysts. I also regularly directly supervised personnel and enjoyed fostering an environment of continual professional growth and development.

Lastly, I am truly passionate about serving my country and, though I will be separating from the military in September, I feel that joining an organization like VK Contract Services would allow me to continue serving by identifying potential threats through data collection and analysis. With this passion for continuing to serve my country as a contractor coupled with my extensive experience in managing intelligence collection operations and training intelligence personnel, I feel that I would be a great fit for the role and hope to start my next career at VK Contract Services.

I look forward to hearing from you.

Sincerely,

Your Name

Cover Letter 4: Transitioning Military

Your Name
Street Address
City, State Zip
555-555-5555
YourEmail@email.com

Date Sending (January 6, 2020 format)

Re: IT Help Desk

Dear Mr. Doe,

I was excited to learn about the IT Help Desk position with Tech Geeks Inc. at the Springfield branch and am writing to inform you of my intention to apply for the position.

I feel that I would be a great fit for this position as I have a Bachelor's degree in Computer Science and over 3 years of experience troubleshooting, diagnosing, and resolving hardware, software, and networking issues for the University of Tennessee's IT Department. I also recently earned the CompTIA A+ Certification and plan to continue independently studying to earn the Network + certification.

Another reason that I feel I'm a great fit for this position is that I enjoy assisting end-users in resolving technical issues. I find the task of finding and fixing technical errors or issues to be a fun challenge and as such, I consistently receive high praise from supervisors for completing trouble-tickets quickly and efficiently while receiving high ratings on customer satisfaction surveys.

Lastly, I wholeheartedly agree with Tech Geeks' organizational mission of making customers' lives easier by "taking the frustration out of tech." I would truly enjoy working for Tech Geeks and making customer's lives easier by resolving their technical issues and feel that my passion for assisting customers paired with my ample technical assistance experience make me the ideal candidate for the IT Help Desk position.

I look forward to hearing from you.

Sincerely,

Your Name

Cover Letter 5: General Cover Letter

Resume Examples

Rather than come up with a fake client name for each of these resume examples, I've listed the industry or field that the resume is written toward in the spot where your name would be written. Hopefully, you'll find an example here for your field that will help you build a strong resume that lands you your next job!

And as with the cover letter examples, feel free to use the information from these resume examples word for word in your own resume!

ADMINISTRATIVE ASSISTANT

Waynesburg, PA, 15370 | 555-555-5555 | email@email.com

SUMMARY OF QUALIFICATIONS

Administrative Assistant with an Associate's degree in Business Administration and over 8 years of experience providing bookkeeping and administrative support. Proven track record in processing payroll, invoices, and accounts payable and receivable while tracking all financial operations in QuickBooks. Experienced in office management with responsibility for facilitating smooth daily office operations and managing equipment and office supply inventories. Regularly improve office efficiency by assessing administrative or document management procedures and applying innovative technologies which increase office productivity.

KEY SKILLS

Administration & Scheduling | Calendar Management | Customer Service | Documentation & Filing | Data Entry
Account Management | CRM Systems | Office Inventory Management | Billing & Reconciliations

PROFESSIONAL EXPERIENCE

Officer Manager & Administrative Assistant   May 2016 – January 2020
Pitt Construction, Pittsburgh, PA

- Managed a construction company home office and provided clerical support for 5 project managers including the maintenance of administrative and bookkeeping documents.
- Implemented the use of cloud document storage to improve accessibility for project managers in the field which increased the speed of permit authorizations.
- Maintained purchase logs, change logs, and contracts for multiple projects simultaneously.
- Managed the inventory of office supplies and equipment, ordering replacement supplies as needed.
- Answered a multiline phone, scheduled appointments, and coordinated project managers' calendars.

Administrative Assistant & Bookkeeper   April 2012 – May 2016
Pittsburgh Steel, Pittsburgh, PA

- Managed and maintained account ledgers using QuickBooks, recording financial transactions, reconciling monthly invoices and bank or credit accounts, and creating monthly financial reports.
- Processed bi-weekly payroll for 35 employees, monitoring hours worked, deducting appropriate state and federal taxes, and completing payments using direct deposit.
- Spearheaded a company-wide transition from hardcopy documents to an all-electronic document system with responsibility for training the administrative staff across 4 sites to correctly use the new system.
- Communicated with external vendors and other agencies to request invoice completion or reconcile any payment or product issues.

Bank Teller   September 2010 – April 2012
Money Bank, Monaca, PA

- Accurately processed deposits, withdrawals, loan payments, cashier's checks, and stop payments.
- Balanced each day's transactions, verifying cash totals and reporting any issues to management.
- Greeted all patrons and provided a positive customer experience, answering questions, looking up account information, and informing patrons of products, services, or ongoing promotions.
- Received employee of the month 5 times during tenure for providing stellar customer service.

EDUCATION & SPECIALIZED TRAINING

- Associate of Arts, Business Administration, Community College of Beaver County, Monaca, PA, December May 2012
- QuickBooks Training Course, New Horizons Computer Center, Pittsburgh, PA, May 2012

Administrative Assistant

ATHLETIC TRAINER

555.555.5555 ♦ email@gmail.com

SUMMARY OF QUALIFICATIONS

Certified Athletic Trainer with 3 years of experience providing injury evaluations, treatment, and rehabilitation. Proven track record in developing communicative and relationships with coaches and athletes. Experienced in providing emergency response and acute care across a variety of student athletic sports. Regularly develop individualized or group preventative care plans in collaboration with physicians and coaches. Experienced in managing the budget, inventory, and maintenance for equipment and supplies. Regularly track and analyze injury data and information from wearable technology to identify reoccurring injuries and create progress reports. Possess a Master's in Athletic Training and MO Athletic Training licensure.

CORE SKILLS

Sports Medicine ♦ Injury Evaluation & Treatment ♦ Evidence-Based Practices ♦ Relationship Development
Budgeting & Grant Writing ♦ Data Analysis & Reports ♦ Wearable Technology ♦ Emergency Response

EDUCATION & CERTIFICATIONS

- Master of Athletic Training, University of Missouri, Columbia, MO, May 2016
- Bachelor of Science, Exercise & Sports Science, Texas State University, San Marcos, TX, May 2013
- Certified Athletic Trainer (ATC), Board of Certification, ID: BOC 5555555, Expires: December 2023
- Athletic Training Licensure (MLAT), State of Missouri, Issued: 2016
- CPR for the Health Care Provider, American Heart Association, Expires: April 2021

PROFESSIONAL EXPERIENCE

Athletic Trainer   August 2018 – Present
Truman University, Kirksville, MO
- Provide sports medicine coverage including emergency response, acute care, injury evaluations, treatment, and rehabilitation using evidence-based practices for over 200 athletes across 8 sports teams.
- Create individual and group preventative programs with athletes, coaches, and other medical staff.
- Manage an equipment and supplies budget and write grant applications to fund the purchase wearable technology and associated software.
- Implement data-driven practices to determine the root cause of injuries, maintaining statistics on trends to identify reoccurring injuries and provide progress reports.

Assistant Athletic Trainer (Contract)   September 2017 – September 2018
University of Missouri-Kansas City, Kansas City, MO
- Assisted the University's Sports Medicine Staff with special events, tournaments, and games as needed.
- Provided emergency response, wound care, and acute injury evaluations for a large collegiate volleyball tournament, monitoring 4 volleyball courts being used simultaneously and assessing athlete's for injury.
- Utilized a data management system to track athlete injuries and rehabilitative progress.
- Communicated with coaches, physicians, and athletes to convey the severity of athlete's injuries and ensure all treatment plans were followed to avoid further injury.

Professional Clinical Rotations:
- **High School Track**, Rock Bridge Senior High School, Columbia, MO, January 2016 – May 2016
- **Division I College Football**, University of Missouri, Columbia, MO, January 2015 – December 2015
- **High School Football & Volleyball**, David H. Hickman High School, Columbia, MO, August 2014– December 2014

Athletic Trainer

CUSTOMER SERVICE

Morgantown, WV 26504 ♦ 555.555.5555 ♦ email@email.com

SUMMARY OF QUALIFICATIONS

Customer service professional currently completing an Associate's degree in Business Administration with experience in retail, billing, and call center environments. Proven track record in creating, organizing, and filing documents in hardcopy or electronic formats. Regularly provide a quality customer service experience for both internal and external customers in person, by phone, or via email. Experienced in maintaining an inventory of products and supplies, monitoring supply levels, and conducting inspections to remove defective or expired items. Regularly communicate with teammates and collaborate with external agencies to complete projects.

CORE COMPETENCIES

Administration & Scheduling ♦ Quality Customer Service ♦ Documentation Management ♦ Conflict Resolution
Inventory & Supply Management ♦ Communication ♦ Policy Compliance ♦ Sales Transactions

PROFESSIONAL EXPERIENCE

Administrative Assistant February 2018 – January 2020
West Virginia University, Morgantown, WV
- Scheduled appointments, conference calls, and meetings for 10 office personnel, coordinating their schedules and setting automatic staff reminders as needed.
- Created, distributed, and maintained office documentation in both paper and hardcopy formats.
- Monitored and inventoried office supply levels, identifying office supply needs and submitting supply orders on a monthly basis.

Customer Service Representative March 2016 – December 2018
WVU Medical Center, Morgantown, WV
- Provided customer service support for up to 45 customers per day in a fast-paced call center environment, answering phones, providing information on unpaid accounts, and answering customer questions as able.
- Created and sent invoices, bills, and late payment notices by mail or email for services rendered.
- Processed check, credit, or cash payments, ensuring accuracy of totals before completing transactions.

Sales Associate June 2015 – February 2016
Hot Topic, Elkins, WV
- Completed sales transactions using a Point of Sales system and processed cash, credit, or check transactions.
- Assisted customers in locating desired merchandize, answering questions as able and directing customers to the online store in order to fulfill their need for products not within the physical store.
- Conducted product inventories, identifying missing or damaged items and creating loss reports for manager.

Customer Service Associate May 2013 – June 2015
Elkin Cinemas 8, Elkins, WV
- Greeted customers entering the theatre complex and completed sales transactions for movie tickets.
- Completed sales for candy, beverages, and snacks, preparing food items in accordance with company policies while complying with FDA food safety regulations.
- Answered customer questions and resolved any complaints to maintain customer satisfaction.
- Inventoried perishable food supplies, monitoring supply levels and reporting the need to order more items.

EDUCATION

- (Currently) Associate of Arts, Business Administration, West Virginia University, Morgantown, WV, Estimated Graduation, May 2020
- High School Diploma, Elkins High School, Elkins, WV, May 2015

Customer Service

Cybersecurity

Seattle, WA 98105 ♦ 555-555-5555 ♦ Email@email.com

SUMMARY OF QUALIFICATIONS

Cybersecurity analyst with a Master's in Cybersecurity Engineering, a top secret clearance, and experience providing information security and support for multimillion-dollar systems. Proven track record in identifying information assurance risks and conducting penetration testing to determine system vulnerabilities. Experienced in researching and recommending more effective systems to protect an organization's secure documents and customer data. Regularly collaborate with cross-functional groups across the organization to enhance information security processes. Experienced in creating comprehensive system reports to brief executive leadership on major vulnerabilities and system threats. Possess the CompTIA Security + and Cybersecurity Analyst certifications.

CORE COMPETENCIES

Security Systems Infrastructure ♦ Hardware/Software Implementation ♦ Strategic Planning ♦ Risk Management
Data Analysis ♦ Configuration Management ♦ Security Audits ♦ Incident Reporting ♦ Penetration Testing

TECHNICAL SKILLS

Applications: Microsoft Office 2007/2010/2013, Active Directory, Server Manager, Putty, Security Onion, Backtrack/Kali, Wireshark, Metasploit, Nessus, IBM QRadar, IBM Bigfix, Netbrain, PhishBait, Efficient IP

Systems: Windows Server 2012, Windows 10/8/7/Vista/XP/2000, Cisco 3500 Series Switches, Cisco 2900 Series Routers, VMware Workstation 11 and 12, Apache Web Server, Ubuntu, Fedora, CentOS, Debian

Hardware: Linksys Routers, Switches, Hubs, Notebooks, Workstations, Modems, Network Interface Cards, Graphics Cards, Sound Cards, Memory, Hard Drives, Printers, Scanners

PROFESSIONAL EXPERIENCE

Cybersecurity Analyst   June 2018 – January 2019
Money Bank, Seattle, WA

- Reviewed and analyzed logs generated within the network, managed anti-malware applications, and evaluated vulnerability scans to make recommendations for remediation priorities.
- Scheduled and documented the testing of the Disaster Recovery and Business Continuity Program.
- Identified more effective information security programs, recommended new programs and/or systems to management, and spearheaded the roll-out of new security programs for over 1,500 internal users.
- Created and maintained documents and reports in an electronic database to track and record real-time system attacks and potential attacks.
- Participated in the interpretation, revision, distribution, and enforcement of IT Security Policies.
- Defined, analyzed, evaluated, and provided process oversight for the implementation of security solutions and operational security tools to meet business needs.

Information Security Analyst   December 2014 – May 2018
Department of Public Safety, Seattle, WA

- Monitored cybersecurity events requiring focused response, containment, investigation, and remediation with a team of 4 other analysts.
- Collected and analyzed event information, performed threat or target analysis, and facilitated the tracking, handling, and reporting of all security incidents in accordance with department policies.
- Selected by management to produce technical, operational, and executive level reports on security events and incidents and provided oral briefs to executive leadership on major incidents.
- Managed firewall, web content filtering, secure email gateways, intrusion prevention systems, intrusion detection systems, and proxy services.

Cybersecurity Page 1

Information Technology Support (Internship)   December 2013 – December 2014
Tacoma Public Works, Tacoma, WA
- Conducted research to identify, develop, and apply improved methods for the protection of Information Technology systems with in-depth analysis to determine the efficiency of new methods.
- Tested security methods and systems to prevent or limit the loss of IT resources due to unauthorized access, destruction, disclosure, tampering, or alteration.
- Studied the performance of IT systems' vulnerabilities while determining proposed solutions.
- Developed comprehensive system reports and briefed management on recommended security tools.
- Instructed internal personnel on the proper application of IT security techniques and assisted in troubleshooting, diagnosing, and resolving hardware, software, or security issues.

IT Tier I Service Assistant (Contract)   December 2011 – December 2013
TekSystems (St. Joseph's Medical Center), Tacoma, WA
- Monitored requests in an electronic trouble-ticket system and responded first to top priority requests.
- Delivered a quality customer service interaction with end-users in person, by phone, or via email and received an employee of the year award for providing top-notch customer service during all calls.
- Troubleshot, diagnosed, and repaired or resolved hardware, software, system, and/or network issues.
- Maintained detailed documentation regarding service calls in a trouble-ticket system and ensured all open tickets were completed within organizational timelines.
- Maintained over $500,000 of inventory, specialized equipment, and supplies, conducting periodic inspections of equipment across multiple sites to identify, repair, and/or replace defective items.

EDUCATION & CERTIFICATIONS

Master of Science, Cybersecurity Engineering, University of Washington, Bothell, WA, May 2014

Bachelor of Science, Cybersecurity & Networking, Green River College, Auburn, WA, December 2011

Certifications

CompTIA Cybersecurity Analyst, August 2015
Security +, CompTIA, July 2014
Network +, CompTIA, January 2014
A+, CompTIA, February 2012

Cybersecurity Page 2

ELECTRICIAN

555.555.5555 ♦ email@gmail.com

SUMMARY OF QUALIFICATIONS

Licensed Master Electrician with over 10 years of experience in the installation, removal, and/or repair of electrical systems and equipment. Proven track record in adhering to applicable codes and regulations for commercial, industrial, and residential environments. Regularly manage a small team of journeyman electricians and helpers, delegating tasks during projects and providing constructive feedback to foster career growth. Experienced in troubleshooting and repairing existing electrical systems or equipment. Regularly provide a quality customer service interaction while gathering information regarding electrical issues and providing cost estimates.

CORE SKILLS

Electrical Installation ♦ Emergency Repairs ♦ NEC & Local Codes ♦ Troubleshooting & Diagnosis ♦ Safety
Project Estimates ♦ Customer Service ♦ Crew Supervision ♦ Equipment Maintenance ♦ Blueprints & Schematics

LICENSURE & EDUCATION

Master Electrician License, State of Maine, 2013

Journeyman Electrician License, State of Maine, May 2009

Electrician Technology Certificate, Southern Maine Community College, South Portland, ME, May 2008

PROFESSIONAL EXPERIENCE

Master Electrician   March 2014 – January 2020
Electric Wrench Co., Bangor, ME

- Supervised a crew of 6 personnel consisting of 3 electricians and 3 helpers during the installation or troubleshooting and repair of large and small electrical projects.
- Spoke with customers and clients to determine the scope of the project and visited work sites to determine equipment and labor needs before providing a project cost estimate.
- Collaborated with the company owner to create more efficient crews by teaming an electrician with a helper for each project which sped up completion rates and improved customer satisfaction.
- Conducted quality control reviews on all completed projects to ensure adherence to NEC and local codes before determining projects to be finished.
- Installed electrical systems and equipment in industrial and commercial settings during the construction process and on existing structures.

Journeyman Electrician   May 2009 – February 2014
Electrify It Right LLC, Portland, ME

- Performed the installation of ¾" to 4" EMT, PVC, and RGS conduit in accordance with NEC and local codes.
- Pulled wires such as #12 to 500 MCM and set panels, switchboards, and other electrical equipment for 120/208v and 277/480v systems.
- Properly installed general residential lighting, high-end decorative lighting, and commercial lighting systems as requested by clients.
- Read, interpreted, and followed contract drawings, specifications, blueprints, and other schematics as needed to complete electrical projects.
- Maintained an inventory of electrical equipment, tools, parts, and supplies and operated a company vehicle while adhering to all rules of the road.

Electrician Page 1

Apprentice Electrician   June 2008 – May 2009
John Doe & Sons Electric, South Portland, ME
- Gained experience in the installation and troubleshooting of Fire Alarm systems in both commercial and industrial settings.
- Under the supervision of the Master Electrician, reviewed system and interconnection design for adherence to Electrical Code (NEC) and industry best practices.
- Performed system commissioning and function checks to ensure all electrical systems properly functioned and were safe for client use.
- Assisted with the creation of installation reports and regularly determined project cost estimates.
- Maintained an organized and clean company vehicle with all required tools and equipment to complete electrical projects.

Electrician Helper   May 2007 – May 2008
John Doe & Sons Electric, South Portland, ME
- Ensured all necessary materials and tools arrived at each job site and cleaned up job sites after each day of work in residential settings to ensure a safe living space for the customer.
- Followed all electricians' directions and assisted in pulling wire and installing electrical outlets and switches as needed.
- Operated company vehicles including a van and box truck to deliver materials and equipment to various electrical project sites.

Electrician Page 2

EMERGENCY MANAGEMENT

Louisville, KY 40041 ♦ 555-555-5555 ♦ email@email.com

SUMMARY OF QUALIFICATIONS

Emergency Management professional with a Master's in Safety, Security, and Emergency Management and experience creating emergency response plans and training programs. Proven track record in providing instruction and facilitating live exercises and emergency drills for a variety of threats. Experienced in managing and coordinating major projects in collaboration with local, state, or federal agencies. Regularly developed, coordinated, and facilitated the appropriate evaluation and response to control hazardous materials and mitigate loss of life or property damage. Experienced in creating, organizing, and maintaining documentation and records using a computer database. Able to conduct in-depth emergency preparedness analysis in order to create comprehensive corrective action reports. Possess the Federal Emergency Management certification.

CORE COMPETENCIES

Emergency Management ♦ Data Analysis ♦ Reports & Documentation ♦ Inventory & Resource Management
Risk Management ♦ Safety Compliance ♦ Instruction & Training ♦ Project Management ♦ Strategic Planning

PROFESSIONAL EXPERIENCE

Emergency Management & Safety Manager   June 2017 – January 2020
Wildcat Healthcare, Louisville, KY
- Developed or updated short- and long-term emergency response policies for the organization in order to increase staff and patient safety in case of a natural emergency or terroristic threat.
- Gathered and created presentation materials before facilitating a company-wide required training on the appropriate responses to a variety of emergencies.
- Collaborated with the building's Facilities Manager and the city's code enforcement officials to conduct a complete building inspection, identify issues, and correct any failures to adhere to safety regulations.
- Reviewed emergency response procedures during fire drills in order to identify any gaps in operations and worked closely with healthcare administration managers to improve staff and patient safety.
- Identified a gap in preparedness for pandemic response procedures and partnered with the CDC to provide training to all hospital staff at all levels of the organization.

Emergency Response Program Assistant   November 2014 – May 2017
We Respond LLC, Lexington, KY
- Contracted with local towns, businesses, and community organizations to assess each organization's needs, identify potential natural or man-made threats, and create tailored emergency response plans.
- Reviewed the exterior and interior of sites, noting points of emergency egress and the placement of fire suppression equipment to create comprehensive corrective action plans for a variety of organizations.
- Coordinated and facilitated fire drills, tornado drills, and active shooter response drills with large and small groups of staff to test the organization's existing plans or test an updated plan.
- Selected above peers to train incoming personnel on organizational policies and procedures.

Kentucky State Trooper   October 2010 – November 2014
Kentucky Highway Patrol, Lexington, KY
- Enforced traffic laws, apprehended traffic law violators, and investigated rural traffic accidents.
- Assisted other officers during various emergencies and collaborated with multiple agencies on multi-level emergency crises such as fires, natural disasters, or hostage situations.
- Collected and entered data or witness statements in an electronic database for civil or criminal cases.
- Recovered stolen vehicles or property, apprehending wanted persons in accordance with state laws.

Emergency Management Page 1

Security Officer   May 2008 – January 2010
Kentucky State Penitentiary, Eddyville, KY
- Assisted in the development of new prisoner transport procedures which decreased prisoner infractions and minimized the potential for escape.
- Provided security to several areas of a state prison and ensured the safety of all staff and prisoners.
- Communicated clearly with security staff, onsite counselors, and medical staff to provide information regarding prisoner health and convey any safety issues prisoners might pose.
- Regularly called upon by senior officers to deescalate tense or hostile situations with prisoners.

EDUCATION & SPECIALIZED TRAINING

- Master of Science, Safety, Security, & Emergency Management, Eastern Kentucky University, Frankfurt, KY, May 2014
- Bachelor of Applied Science, Emergency Management & Homeland Security, Arizona State University, Tempe, AZ, May 2012
- Federal Emergency Management Certification, Emergency Management Institute, June 2014
- Certified Safety Professional (CSP), Board of Certified Safety Professionals, July 2015

Federal Emergency Management Agency (FEMA) Courses:
- Introduction to Incident Command System ICS-10
- Emergency Planning
- Communications & Information Management
- Introduction to Incident Command System ICS-100 for Federal Workers, School, Public Work, Law Enforcement, Healthcare/Hospital, Higher Education, and Food & Drug Administration
- NIMS Multi-Agency Coordination System (MACS)
- NIMS Resource Management
- National Response Framework
- National Incident Management System (NIMS)

Emergency Management Page 2

EMPLOYMENT SERVICES SPECIALIST

Danbury, CT 06811 | (555) 555-5555 | email@email.com | LinkedIn Profile Link

SUMMARY OF QUALIFICATIONS

Employment Specialist with a Master's in Career Counseling and over 7 years of career development and coaching experience. Proven track record in connecting job seekers to appropriate employment or educational programs. Regularly create and facilitate career-focused workshops and seminars on resume writing, interview preparation, and LinkedIn profile creation. Experienced in administering career, personality, and vocational interest assessments, interpreting results, and discussing information with clients. Regularly conduct outreach activities at community events in order to build organizational awareness and gain more clients. Experienced in creating and maintaining data in a customer relationship management (CRM) system to track client progress.

RELEVANT SKILLS

Civilian & Federal Resumes | LinkedIn Profile | Interview Preparation | Job Search Strategies | Coaching
Client Intake | Instruction & Training | CRM Systems | Program Outreach | Workshops & Seminars

PROFESSIONAL EXPERIENCE

Employment Services Specialist   July 2016 – January 2020
Hiring Our Heroes, Danbury, CT
- Connected over 130 veterans and family support members to employment through assistance in resume writing, interview practice, salary negotiation, and best networking practices.
- Created relationships with employers and recruiters, explaining the merits of hiring veteran and family members and discussing possible workplace accommodations.
- Represented the organization at career fairs, state agency meetings, and local nonprofit meetings, explaining the organization's employment services and other programs.
- Facilitated 40 workshops for veterans, family members, employers, and other service organizations.
- Managed a caseload of 145 clients simultaneously and tracked progress via a computer database.

Transition Counselor   July 2013 – July 2016
Soldier for Life Transition Assistance Program, Fort Worth, TX
- Provided career counseling services to transitioning service members and assessed each soldier's education and work experience to compare with his or her career goals.
- Created resumes, LinkedIn profiles, and individual transition plans to ensure career readiness.
- Conducted career-oriented seminars and workshops, including federal resume writing, personality assessment, and the use of social media for employment seeking purposes.
- Engaged in one-on-one counseling with soldiers to create short and long-term career goals, following up with soldiers to track progress on goal completion.
- Regularly connected with soldiers throughout the transition life cycle, touching base before transition, around soldier's transition date, and again 6 months after separation from the military.
- Represented the company at career fairs and liaised with external organizations to gain client referrals.

Career Counselor (Intern)   September 2010 – May 2011
West Virginia University Career Center, Morgantown, WV
- Provided individual and group career counseling sessions for current students and university alumni.
- Conducted personality and career assessments to assist clients in identifying their vocational interests.
- Assessed each client's education, work history, and professional accomplishments in order to provide informed and realistic suggestions for immediate employment.
- Identified clients' career goals and discussed steps toward gaining the education or experience needed.

EDUCATION

- **Master of Arts**, Career Counseling, West Virginia University, Morgantown, WV, 2011
- **Bachelor of Science**, Psychology, Middle Tennessee State University, Murfreesboro, TN, 2008

Employment Services Specialist

HEALTHCARE ADMINISTRATION

Boston, MA 02111 | 555-555-5555 | email@email.com

SUMMARY OF QUALIFICATIONS

Healthcare professional with a Master's degree in Healthcare Administration and 5 years of experience managing regulatory compliance for both public and private hospitals. Proven track record in developing and facilitating training for nurses, physicians, and administrative staff to improve individual performance and increase patient safety. Experienced in implementing the adoption of an electronic medical records database to more efficiently and confidentially manage patient records. Regularly collaborate across all levels of an organization and analyze data and hospital metrics to identify process or performance issues and develop solutions.

KEY SKILLS

Risk Management | Healthcare Training & Instruction | Data Analysis | Quality Control | Patient Safety
Supply Inventory Control | Medical Records Management | Performance Improvement | Regulatory Compliance

EDUCATION & SPECIALIZED TRAINING

- Certified Medical Manager (CMM), Professional Association of Healthcare Office Management (PAHCOM), December 2015
- Master of Public Health (MPH), Providence College, Providence, RI, May 2015
- Bachelor of Science, Healthcare Administration, Husson University, Bangor, ME, May 2012

PROFESSIONAL EXPERIENCE

Administrative Manager   December 2017 – January 2019
Boston Hospital, Boston, MA

- Managed the operations, human resources, finances, strategic planning, and project management for an oncology department while adhering to the hospital's core values of providing outstanding clinical care.
- Conducted a survey of patients and healthcare staff which uncovered after-care issues and increased customer and employee satisfaction by creating a Patient Liaison position focused solely on aftercare.
- Directly managed 12 personnel including 4 divisional managers, providing support as needed and ensuring each employee's performance met or exceeded organizational expectations.
- Developed a relationship with a local university and was awarded a federal grant to hire healthcare information systems interns and implement a more patient-accessible medical records database.
- Maintained records regarding the appropriate licensing and certification of all staff members and provided email or verbal reminders to renew any certifications that were soon-to-expire.

Healthcare Operations Manager   May 2015 – November 2017
Urgent Care Centers of Boston, Boston, MA

- Advised the Medical Treatment Facility Director on policies and procedures that impacted the measurement of workload and on issues concerning the utilization of resources.
- Evaluated healthcare delivery systems and operations, implementing efforts to improve the systems and processes affecting the speed and accuracy of patient assistance.
- Supervised 8 medical staff and provided performance evaluations, corrective counseling, and suggestions for professional development to foster career growth.
- Managed a $2 million yearly budget for payroll, equipment, and medical supplies, conducting a quarterly analysis on spending trends in order to forecast future purchases and hiring capabilities.
- Oversaw the delivery of $5 million in healthcare services for over 35,000 patients and ensured all patients received a safe and quality experience.

Healthcare Administration Page 1

Health & Safety Manager   June 2012 – May 2015

Memorial Hospital, Boston, MA

- Led the organization's accident and injury prevention program which ensured compliance with local, state, and federal regulations.
- Conducted incident investigations and root cause analysis in collaboration with the Human Resources Department to develop recommendations for actions to prevent accident or injury recurrence.
- Coordinated and facilitated an organization-wide safety training brief required for all staff which resulted in an immediate decrease of onsite accidents.
- Developed a more engaging new hire safety orientation and updated other existing safety training programs to better reflect the reality of hospital incidents and accidents.
- Managed a $150,000 budget and made all purchasing decisions on safety-related supplies or equipment.

Assistant Health & Safety Manager   April 2008 – June 2012

Moose Manufacturing, Bangor, ME

- Identified and assisted in the design, development, and execution of Environmental Health and Safety policies, guidelines, procedures, and programs
- Conducted site safety training in a group setting and provided individual training for specific equipment such as forklifts and press machines, certifying staff and maintaining their training records.
- Provided direct support in risk management analysis, identifying potential injury risks and developing resolutions to mitigate or eliminate the risk factor.
- Maintained all documentation for a site incident prevention program (SIPP) and spearheaded the migration from a paper filing system to an all-electronic system which increased speed of data recall.

Healthcare Administration Page 2

INTELLIGENCE ANALYST MANAGER
Clarksville, TN 37043
555-555-5555 • email@email.com

SUMMARY OF QUALIFICATIONS

U.S. Army Special Forces Veteran with a Bachelor of Business Administration and over 10 years of experience in data collection and analysis. Proven track record in the use of complex software systems to collect, analyze, and compile data into comprehensive reports for presentation to senior executives. Experienced in managing large, multimillion-dollar projects and supervising cross-functional teams in remote locations on a global scale. Regularly collaborate with external departments, foreign military personnel, and federal agencies to complete projects within assigned deadlines. Possess a Top Secret Security Clearance with CI Poly.

RELEVANT SKILLS

Project Management • Data Analysis & Presentation • Organizational Development • Communication
ArcGIS Mapping • Training & Development • Strategic Planning • Policies & Regulations

PROFESSIONAL EXPERIENCE

Intelligence Planning & Operations Manager   September 2015 – Present
U.S. Army Special Forces, Fort Campbell, KY & Tampa, FL
- Directly managed 4 junior intelligence analysts and coordinated collaboration with analysts from federal agencies to ensure adherence to appropriate data collection and analysis policies.
- Coordinated training and operations for a 400-person element resulting in the completion of 42 training events and 21 overseas operations.
- Conducted quarterly and annual performance evaluations for 10 personnel and provided corrective counseling as necessary.
- Validated over 80 risk management assessments, ensuring the risk mitigation factors were realistic and enforceable.
- Directly responsible for over $8.6 million worth of specialized military equipment and identified over $2 million worth of extraneous equipment for reallocation.
- Applied conceptual and standardized planning techniques to develop regional operational strategies that nested with strategic level goals.

Intelligence Analyst & Supervisor   August 2010 – September 2015
U.S. Army Special Forces, Fort Campbell, KY, Iraq, & Afghanistan
- Compiled and analyzed raw intelligence from multiple sources using data mining research techniques and intelligence software that led to the successful completion of 100 operations.
- Planned local and global operations from concept to implementation while adhering to national level policy and regulation.
- Developed and managed a $250,000 budget to procure critical equipment and fund individual and collective training which led to a 100% training completion rate.
- Authored comprehensive briefs and created presentations for small military teams and/or groups of executive level leadership.
- Trained personnel in the use of digital photography, audio, and video surveillance to collect data as well as ArcGIS software for compiling and mapping intelligence information.

Intelligence Analyst Manager Page 1

Construction & Demolition Engineer   August 2007 – August 2010
U.S. Army Special Forces, Fort Campbell, KY & Iraq

- Completed demolition operations on bridges, railroads, and other infrastructure while adhering to all safety policies and procedures.
- Employed tactics and techniques during overseas operations in order to complete team projects.
- Interpreted maps, overlays, photos, and charts to determine if demolition was required to complete the organization's objective.
- Managed the logistics for a small team of military personnel to prepare for deployment to overseas locations.

Surveillance Technician   September 2003 – August 2007
U.S. Army, Fort Sill, OK & Afghanistan

- Set up all equipment to conduct surveillance projects in remote, austere locations and gathered intelligence and information on specific subjects.
- Inventoried and maintained over $1 million in specialized surveillance equipment.
- Trained 2 personnel in the appropriate procedures for setting up surveillance to gain maximum information while remaining undetected by subjects.

EDUCATION & SPECIALIZED TRAINING

- Bachelor of Business Administration, American Military University, Charles Town, WV, May 2018
- Senior Leadership (Management & Planning) Course, U.S. Army, Fort Bragg, NC, 2012
- Intelligence Collection & Analysis Training, U.S. Army Special Forces, Fort Bragg, NC, 2011
- Construction & Demolition Course, U.S. Army Special Forces, Fort Bragg, NC, 2007

Intelligence Manager Page 2

IT Help Desk Technician

Bristol, CT 06010 ♦ 555-555-5555 ♦ Email@email.com

SUMMARY OF QUALIFICATIONS

Information technology help desk technician with a Bachelor's degree in Computer Science and experience providing Tier 1 help desk support for end-users. Proven track record in troubleshooting, diagnosing, and resolving hardware, software, and connectivity issues. Regularly manage projects from concept to completion within assigned timelines. Experienced in providing a positive customer service experience in person, over the phone, and via email. Regularly create, organize, and maintain documentation regarding customer interactions or services provided. Experienced in the inventory and maintenance of equipment, supplies, and materials. Able to communicate across all levels of an organization and possess the A+ CompTIA certification.

CORE COMPETENCIES

Help Desk Support ♦ Administration ♦ Troubleshooting & Diagnosis ♦ Customer Service ♦ Communication
Documentation & Reports ♦ Networking ♦ Inventory & Resource Management ♦ System Security

EDUCATION & SPECIALIZED TRAINING

Bachelor of Science, Computer Science, Eastern Connecticut State University, Willimantic, CT, May 2010

A+ Certification, CompTIA, February 2011

TECHNICAL SKILLS

Operating Systems: Windows 2013/2010/2007/ XP, Windows Server 2008, Linux
Hardware: PCs, laptops, cabling including fiber optics, DSL modems, Wireless cards, USB adapters, Video Cards, Sound Cards
Software: Microsoft Word, Excel, PowerPoint, Outlook
Networking: Subnet Masking, IP Addressing, LAN/WAN, TCP/IP Protocols, Cisco Routers & Switches, GUI Applications, Ethernet Drivers

PROFESSIONAL EXPERIENCE

IT Tier I Service Assistant   November 2016 – December 2019
Bristol Hospital, Bristol, CT

- Monitored requests in an electronic trouble-ticket system and responded first to top priority requests.
- Delivered a quality customer service interaction with end-users in person, by phone, or via email and received an employee of the year award for providing top customer service during all calls.
- Troubleshot, diagnosed, and repaired or resolved hardware, software, system, and/or network issues.
- Maintained detailed documentation regarding service calls in a trouble-ticket system and ensured all open tickets were completed within organizational timelines.
- Maintained over $1million of inventory, specialized equipment, and supplies, conducting periodic inspections of equipment across multiple sites to identify, repair, and/or replace defective items.

Help Desk Technician   January 2013 – November 2016
Electronics Fix It, Willimantic, CT

- Troubleshot, diagnosed, and resolved issues with iPhones, iPads, iPods and other Apple devices.
- Selected by management to oversee the migration to a new Customer Relationship Management system and ensure all information was accurately transferred.
- Interacted with customers to inquire about device issues and documented all services provided.
- Coordinated hardware or software installation and/or configuration with Apple stores or shipped devices directly to Apple for more in-depth repairs.
- Trained new personnel in troubleshooting various Apple products and diagnosing issues.

IT Help Desk Technician Page 1

Geek Squad Associate   June 2010 – January 2013
Best Buy, Willimantic, CT
- Assisted customers in reviewing products onsite and provided information to help customers determine the best possible computer or tablet for their needs.
- Provided technical assistance and troubleshooting in person or by phone for customers with computer, phone, or tablet issues.
- Completed system updates, virus scans, data transfers, document retrieval, and/or hard drive replacements on customer computers.

Computer Lab Assistant (Work Study)   June 2008 – May 2010
Eastern Connecticut State University, Willimantic, CT
- Signed in students wishing to use the computer lab by scanning their student ID and assigning a computer station which had the appropriate software to meet their project needs.
- Provided technical assistance as needed, troubleshooting and resolving system, network, software, or hardware malfunctions.
- Assisted the Information Technology department with a campus-wide IT analysis to identify systems and software which received the least use in order to identify which software to cut and save money.

IT Help Desk Technician Page 2

JOURNEYMAN CARPENTER

Jacksonville, FL 32034 ♦ 555.555.5555 ♦ email@gmail.com

SUMMARY OF QUALIFICATIONS

Versatile Journeyman Carpenter with over 10 years of experience in commercial and industrial construction. Proven track record in assessing project specifications in order to estimate the materials, equipment, and staffing levels required to complete projects within deadline. Regularly communicate with project managers and foremen to provide progress updates. Supervise construction projects and regularly selected by management to spearhead difficult projects. Regularly collaborate with safety staff and crew members to ensure a safe work environment while delivering top-quality construction services. Able to navigate a variety of computer programs and use automated databases such as Utilized Production Planning and Scheduling (PPS).

AREAS OF EXPERTISE

Site & Crew Supervision ♦ Project Estimates ♦ Safety & OSHA Regulations ♦ Commercial & Industrial Projects
Steel & Concrete Forms ♦ Schematics ♦ Building Layouts ♦ Framing ♦ Foundation Systems ♦ Finishing

PROFESSIONAL EXPERIENCE

Journeyman Carpenter & Crew Leader　　　　　　　　　　　May 2014 – December 2019
We Construct Co., Jacksonville, FL

- Acted as assistant foreman, providing supervision on large-scale construction projects, delegating daily tasks, and collaborating with safety staff and project managers to ensure timely project completion.
- Selected to take over the supervision of a $1 million Dental Center construction project which was behind schedule and successfully brought the project back up to speed thereby saving over $50,000 in extra costs.
- Completed heavy-duty commercial construction projects, managing the creation of concrete beams for full-building construction on several Department of Defense projects.
- Assessed blueprints and schematics in comparison to physical construction sites before determining the equipment, materials, and staff levels needed to complete projects within or before project deadlines.
- Ensured all required materials and tools were ordered and accurately delivered to construction sites.
- Communicated with project managers to relay realistic project timelines and provide progress updates.
- Identified staff specialties and delegated assignments to those staff with the best or most appropriate skills.
- Collaborated with local rail transit to create steel forms for a major train depot and communicated closely with field engineers and local utility companies to identify and mitigate any safety issues.

Journeyman Carpenter　　　　　　　　　　　　　　　　　February 2011 – May 2014
Joe Builder LLC, Jacksonville, FL

- Performed journeyman carpentry in commercial and industrial settings, creating building layouts, developing foundation systems, framing wall systems, and completing quality finish work for large-scale projects.
- Reviewed blueprints and applied building codes to determine optimal work procedures and identify project specifications to support job setup activities at all assigned locations.
- Utilized drawings, specifications, and instructions to build, remodel, and repair facilities and structures.
- Ensured a safe work environment for all crew members by adhering to and enforcing OSHA standards.

Shipping Supervisor　　　　　　　　　　　　　　　　　　July 2009 – January 2011
Food & Friends, Boca Raton, FL

- Supervised a team of 15 employees and ensured adherence to all policies and OSHA safety regulations.
- Oversaw the shipment of over $1.25 million worth of perishable food per shift while following United States Department of Agriculture (USDA) standards and policies.
- Planned weekly staff schedules and resolved any issues in order to ensure full production line coverage.
- Conducted performance evaluations and provided corrective counseling to resolve staff performance issues.
- Reviewed shipping records and reports to verify order details, monitor progress, and evaluate performance.
- Developed and implemented departmental safety policies and procedures in conjunction with management.

Journeyman Carpenter Page 1

Senior Construction Worker   September 2007– May 2009
Hammer & Nail Builders, Boca Raton, FL

- Provided leadership and project supervision, assisting the foreman in assigning and delegating work duties for large-scale projects at the local water treatment plant and pumping station.
- Read, interpreted, and planned work based on blueprints and other technical drawings.
- Constructed forms and foundations, poured concrete, and erected scaffolding and ladders.
- Reviewed plans, blueprints, specifications, and construction methods to ensure compliance with requirements, building codes, and safety regulations.
- Examined the quality of finished installations and structures to determine structural soundness and compliance with specifications, codes, and other regulations.
- Followed and enforced safety and standard operating procedures, resulting in a safe work environment.

EDUCATION & SPECIALIZED TRAINING

- (Currently), Bachelor of Science, Construction Management, University of North Florida, Jacksonville, FL, Expected Graduation: May 2022
- Renewable Energy Diploma, Everglades University, Boca Raton, FL, May 2011
  Coursework included National Center for Construction Education & Research (NCCER) Modules: Solar Photovoltaics; Wind Energy; Fundamentals of Wiring; Electrical Theory & Electrical Safety; Conductor Installations; Conductor Terminations & Splices; Intro to OSHA, NEC & NFPA; National Electrical Code; Conductors & Cables; Residential Electrical Services; Project Supervision; Contract & Construction Documents

Journeyman Carpenter Page 2

Logistics Manager

1320 Maple Avenue, Nashville, TN 04102 ♦ (555) 555-5555 ♦ JohnADoe55@gmail.com

SUMMARY OF QUALIFICATIONS

U.S. Navy Veteran with a Bachelor's degree in Supply Chain Management and over 15 years of experience planning, coordinating, and managing logistical operations in local, national, and global environments. Proven track record in analyzing material handling procedures to identify areas of improvement and successfully developed a distribution process which increased productivity by 15% while decreasing costs. Experienced in training and supervising personnel, assigning projects, providing performance evaluations, and fostering an environment of professional development. Regularly manage the receipt, storage, inventory, maintenance, and distribution of over $5 million worth of equipment and materials. Possess the Project Management Professional (PMP) certification.

KEY SKILLS

Program & Project Management ♦ Strategic Planning ♦ Inventory & Resource Management ♦ Logistics & Supply Policy Development ♦ Process Improvement ♦ Supervision & Training ♦ Quality Control ♦ Safety Compliance

PROFESSIONAL EXPERIENCE

Logistics Manager   May 2015 – January 2020
U.S. Navy, Sigonella, Sicily & Jacksonville, FL
- Managed a team of 25 logistics personnel and monitored progress in accomplishing shipments before delivery deadlines which resulted in additional time to re-inspect equipment and review load plans.
- Oversaw the planning, organization, and coordination of transportation requirements for over 2,000 personnel and $55 million worth of equipment and supplies during a critical global operation.
- Directly supervised personnel, delegating tasks, conducting performance evaluations, providing corrective counseling, and identifying professional development opportunities to foster career growth.
- Created Standard Operating Procedures (SOP) to maximize the proficiency of the logistics program and more accurately account for inventory which supported up to 5,000 military personnel.
- Maintained documentation on supply counts, material distribution, and the receipt of supply shipments.

Naval Logistics Instructor   September 2013 – May 2015
U.S. Navy, Great Lakes Naval Training Center, Great Lakes, IL
- Supervised over 50 military personnel and oversaw the application of safety policies, procedures, and regulations during various military training operations.
- Facilitated classroom instruction and field training for up to 50 personnel at one time.
- Analyzed projects to identify the resources and time required to complete objectives before creating timelines, setting a schedule, and delegating assignments to personnel within the department.
- Directed scheduled and unscheduled vehicle and equipment inspections to identify malfunctions or maintenance issues and ensure all items were ready for immediate use.

Medical Supply Supervisor   June 2008 – September 2013
U.S. Navy, Naval Medical Center, San Diego, CA
- Supervised a team of medical supply technicians, delegating daily, weekly, and monthly tasks and monitoring progress toward goals to ensure all department objectives were met within deadlines.
- Oversaw the planning, organization, and coordination for the transport or storage of over 10,000 pieces of medical equipment on a daily basis, conducting periodic quality assurance inspections to mitigate loss.
- Oversaw the safe receipt, handling, storage, and shipment of various equipment, supplies, and materials.
- Created, organized, and maintained detailed documentation via hardcopy and electronic formats regarding supply counts, the distribution of materials, and the receipt of shipments.

Logistics Manager Page 1

Shipping Supervisor   June 2005 – June 2008
U.S. Navy, Jacksonville, FL
- Conducted inventory control for over $2 million worth of military vehicles, equipment, supplies, and materials, monitoring and recording the receipt, storage, shipment, and distribution of items.
- Analyzed the shipping and receiving process, identifying quality control measures to eliminate supply count discrepancies and increase productivity without sacrificing safety.
- Supervised the receipt, storage, and shipment of materials and ensured all operations were performed in accordance with organizational regulations.
- Communicated with personnel at all levels and collaborated with external agencies and vendors to requisition and procure required military equipment.
- Conducted periodic inspections to identify and correct any unsafe storage procedures, removing defective items and ensuring total adherence to safety policies.

EDUCATION & SPECIALIZED TRAINING

- Project Management Professional (PMP) Certification, Project Management Institute, August 2017
- Bachelor of Arts, Supply Chain Management, Michigan State University, Lansing, MI, May 2007

Relevant Military Training:
- Logistics Instructor Training, Naval Military Training Instructor School, U.S. Navy, 2013
- Officer Candidate School (Management & Supervision), Officer Training Command, U.S. Navy, 2007
- Logistics & Administration Training, U.S. Navy, Meridian, MS, 2005

HONORS & AWARDS

- Awarded the Navy Commendation Medal in 2018 for managing the movement of over 2,000 personnel and $55 million worth of military equipment, supplies, and vehicles.
- Received a Letter of Commendation in 2016 from executive leadership for delivering a group teambuilding exercise which increased team collaboration and boosted staff morale.

VOLUNTEER EXPERIENCE

Community Events Director, Team Red, White, and Blue   May 2013 – May 2015
- Coordinated, facilitated, and managed group volunteer opportunities in collaboration with local nonprofit organizations or veteran-related federal and state agencies.
- Led large and small groups of team members in athletic events such as rucking, hiking, and running.
- Managed all logistical aspects of coordinating 2 year-end social events for over 200 team members.

Logistics Manager Page 2

Marketing Manager

Los Angeles, CA 90013 ♦ 555-555-5555 ♦ email@email.com
LinkedIn Profile Link

SUMMARY OF QUALIFICATIONS

Marketing Manager with a Master of Business Administration (MBA) in Marketing Management and experience in product, brand, and content management. Proven track record in developing mutually beneficial partnerships to boost brand awareness and increase sales. Experienced in managing cross-functional teams delegating weekly tasks and creating appropriate performance metrics for each individual team member. Regularly analyze market trends, identifying consumer preferences and competitors' strategies to create data-driven, high-impact marketing strategies. Experienced in promoting special deals or packages and consistently increase product sales revenue year over year through long-term marketing efforts. Able to communicate across all levels of an organization to gain detailed product information and create engaging marketing content.

CORE COMPETENCIES

Project Management ♦ Data-Driven Strategies ♦ Social Media Campaigns ♦ Sales ♦ Brand Management
Market Analysis ♦ Product Launches ♦ Partnership Development ♦ Metrics ♦ SEO Optimization

EDUCATION & SPECIALIZED TRAINING

- Master of Business Administration (MBA), Concentration: Marketing Management, University of California Los Angeles, Los Angeles, CA, May 2016
- Advanced Marketing Management Course, Northwestern University, Evanston, IL, May 2014
- Bachelor of Science, Business Administration with a focus on Marketing, University of Southern California, Los Angeles, CA, December 2013

PROFESSIONAL EXPERIENCE

Marketing Manager   June 2018 – January 2020
Star Power Shoes, Los Angeles, CA

- Planned and organized all promotional activities for new products including web presence, digital advertising, social and other media, trade shows, and marketing materials.
- Managed 8 marketing specialists with different areas of marketing expertise and created Key Performance Indicators (KPI) for each team member in accordance with their area of responsibility.
- Oversaw a $2 million marketing budget, strategically allocating funds across marketing channels that would have the highest impact in building brand awareness within the target market.
- Implemented an advertising initiative tailored to sell older products which doubled retail sales in 1 year.
- Developed a social media campaign which increased overall company sales by 45% and gained brand awareness through free celebrity and influencer endorsements.

Brand Manager   July 2016 – May 2018
Funky Gummies, Los Angeles, CA

- Collaborated with a marketing team of sales and social media specialists to monitor consumer trends, competition, and regulatory issues in order to measure product viability and marketplace appeal.
- Developed a strategic 3-year plan to support continual growth and profitability through the managed staggered launch of a series of products and building upon the success of each product's release.
- Managed product lifecycles including SKU rationalization and Product Excellence Management (PEM).
- Performed competitor analysis and developed defensive/offensive plans with competitor's products.
- Created store promotions and built strategic partnerships which increased brand awareness by 15%.

Marketing Manager Page 1

Marketing Specialist   January 2014 – July 2016
Wealth Management Guys, Los Angeles, CA
- Developed and executed an email marketing program which included segmentation, testing, and deployment and continually evaluated these areas for improvements.
- Evaluated campaign metrics and distributed performance information to the rest of the marketing team and the marketing department's executive management team.
- Maintained marketing automation integration with the Customer Relationship Management (CRM) system by working closely with the IT and customer service departments.
- Analyzed data to deliver actionable insights and suggestions to the marketing team in order to increase customer retention and boost new customer sign-ups.

Sales Representative   May 2012 – January 2014
Supersize Distributors, Los Angeles, CA
- Sold products to various commercial clients through in-person store visits, emails, or cold-calls to store managers or owners.
- Provided detailed product information, explaining wholesale costs, retail value, and expected sales profits, increasing commercial accounts through positive customer service experiences.
- Adhered to all FDA food and beverage safety regulations and maintained all efficiency standards.
- Visited potential retail locations and conducted tastings for retail employees and potential customers.

Marketing Manager Page 2

Mechanic

Fayetteville, NC 28303

555-555-5555 ♦ email@email.com

SUMMARY OF QUALIFICATIONS

U.S. Army Reserves veteran with the ASE certification and extensive experience troubleshooting, diagnosing, and repairing gasoline and diesel vehicles. Proven track record in assessing and improving preventative maintenance programs resulting in more vehicle availability. Regularly manage the inventory of equipment, tools, and repair parts, conducting periodic inspections and ordering replacement parts from internal and external vendors. Experienced in creating and maintaining documents in both electronic and hardcopy formats. Able to collaborate with co-workers or work independently to complete projects within assigned deadlines.

CORE COMPETENCIES

Administration & Reports ♦ Customer Service ♦ Inspection & Quality Control ♦ Safety & Policy Compliance
Inventory & Resource Management ♦ Troubleshooting & Diagnosis ♦ Delivery Services ♦ Communication

PROFESSIONAL EXPERIENCE

Diesel Mechanic   May 2015 – Present
Waste Management, Fayetteville, NC

- Manage a fleet of 11 diesel vehicles, monitoring that all preventative maintenance is performed for each vehicle system as appropriate for the mileage driven.
- Communicate with drivers to identify any potential vehicle issues or malfunctions and immediately inspect vehicles at the first suggestion of issues in order to ensure further damage is not sustained.
- Implemented a preventative maintenance system in the first year of employment which has increased the functionality and availability of vehicles by 15% each year with a current availability rate of 95%.
- Maintain a neat and organized garage and adhere to all OSHA safety regulations including the use of personal protective equipment (PPE).

Automotive Mechanic   February 2013 – May 2015
Oil & Brakes Co., Fayetteville, NC

- Performed preventative maintenance on the engine and brake systems, changing oil, brakes, rotors, calipers, and any required air, oil, or fuel filters.
- Assessed and inspected malfunctioning diesel and gasoline vehicles, troubleshooting, identifying, and resolving issues with a variety of systems such as brakes, hydraulics, engine, fuel, and electrical.
- Named employee of the year in 2013 for consistently meeting and exceeding repair project deadlines.
- Monitored replacement part supply levels, submitting requests for supply refills from a local parts warehouse and ensuring all parts deliveries were accurate.
- Maintained a computer database with customer's information, creating system updates as needed to reflect any repairs completed and note preventative maintenance suggested to customers.

Diesel Mechanic Supervisor   November 2011 – January 2013
U.S. Army Reserves & AMSA, Knoxville, TN

- Supervised up to 20 personnel, delegating tasks, conducting individual evaluations to improve performance, and fostering an environment of professional development.
- Trained and instructed personnel in the safe operation and repair of vehicles and specialized equipment.
- Used technical manuals and specialized tools to diagnose and repair heavy/diesel vehicles.
- Utilized a computer database to track inventory, order parts, and track vehicle maintenance.
- Adhered to all OSHA standards and conducted safety and quality control inspections.

Mechanic Page 1

Diesel Mechanic & Tow Technician   October 2007 – November 2011
U.S. Army Reserves, Knoxville, TN and Iraq
- Supervised the location, removal, and towing of large, malfunctioning military vehicles and/or equipment.
- Troubleshot, diagnosed, and repaired electrical, hydraulic, and general diesel systems.
- Regularly conducted inspections and preventative maintenance on diesel equipment to ensure readiness.
- Inventoried equipment, maintaining electronic and handwritten records of vehicle maintenance.
- Utilized hydraulic lifts and specialized tools to perform maintenance and repairs.
- Received a Certificate of Recognition for continually providing maintenance support to personnel while in a hostile environment during an overseas deployment to Iraq.

EXPERIENCE & SPECIALIZED TRAINING

- Automotive Service Excellence (ASE) Certification, National Institute for Automotive Service, May 2015
- Foundation Instructor Facilitator Course (FIFIC), U.S. Army, Fort Leonard Wood, MO, 2012
- Heavy Equipment Diesel Mechanic Course, U.S. Army, Fort Lee, VA, 2011
- Recovery Operation (Towing) Course, U.S. Army, Fort Lee, VA, 2011

Mechanic Page 2

Mental Health Counseling

55 Evans Lane, Biloxi, MS 39530
555-555-5555 ♦ email@email.com

SUMMARY OF QUALIFICATIONS

Behavioral health professional with a Master's in Mental Health Counseling and experience in group, couples, individual, and crisis counseling. Proven track record in case management, maintaining records, and managing archival systems in accordance with HIPAA regulations. Experienced in developing rapport with clients and providing a quality customer service experience in person and over the phone. Regularly administered assessments and assisted clients in identifying mental health barriers before developing individual treatment plans with realistic goals. Experienced in training and supervising clinical interns. Able to build collaborative relationships with community organizations as external resources for clients. Licensed to practice counseling and qualified as a clinical supervisor in Mississippi.

CORE COMPETENCIES

Clinical Counseling & Diagnosis ♦ Case Management ♦ Records Management ♦ Inpatient & Outpatient
Intake & Assessments ♦ Intern Supervision ♦ Community Resource Development ♦ Treatment Teams

EDUCATION & SPECIALIZED TRAINING

- Master of Science, Mental Health Counseling, Mississippi College, Clinton, MS, May 2010
- Cognitive Behavioral Certification, Beck Institute, June 2011
- EMDR Basic Training, Hope Enrichment Center, Southaven, MS, August 2012

LICENSES

- Licensed Professional Counselor (LPC), State of MS, Issued: May 2012, License #: 55-5555
- Mississippi Qualified Supervisor, State of MS, Issued: July 2016

PROFESSIONAL EXPERIENCE

Behavioral Health Clinician   May 2017 – January 2020
Healthy Life Services, Biloxi, MS

- Delivered mental health counseling both in person and via video-feed, diagnosing clients as appropriate, creating individual treatment plans with client input, and providing therapeutic counseling to meet goals.
- Provided consultation and recommendations regarding the implementation of a telehealth division to deliver virtual mental healthcare services for clients nationwide.
- Facilitated the delivery of preventative behavioral health services to over 1,500 clients through interactive modules as a contract for a major health insurance provider.
- Supervised clinical counseling interns, sitting in on counseling sessions, providing feedback after sessions, and addressing any issues or difficulties the interns encountered.
- Maintained case notes in an electronic records database while adhering to all HIPAA rules and regulations.

Mental Health Technician   August 2014 – April 2017
Mississippi State Prison, Biloxi, MS

- Facilitated 3 group counseling sessions with up to 12 clients each with a focus on behavior modification, substance abuse, and dealing with trauma and hopelessness.
- Provided individual counseling as needed with a focus on cognitive-behavioral therapy.
- Created, maintained, and updated electronic mental health records and provided information to security officers regarding each client's ability to socialize with other prisoners or participate in group events.
- Participated in clinical treatment team meeting with a psychiatrist, nurse staff, occupational therapist, and a recreational therapist to discuss each client's ongoing treatment and progress.

Mental Health Counseling Page 1

Mental Health Counselor   May 2010 – August 2014
Mississippi College Student Health Services, Clinton, MS
- Conducted client intake and administered personality or other assessments as needed to determine student's mental health needs.
- Created Individual Treatment Plans (ITPs) with student input regarding mental health goals and set achievable milestones for determining each student's mental health treatment progress.
- Facilitated psycho-educational groups for students on dealing with stress and identifying depression, anxiety, or suicidal behavior.
- Provided crisis counseling and developed a relationship with a local inpatient clinic in order to transfer clients who needed more intensive mental health assistance.

Readjustment Counselor Intern   January 2010 – May 2010
Veteran's Administration (VA) Vet Center, Clinton, MS
- Conducted individual, couples, group and/or crisis counseling sessions for veterans with Post Traumatic Stress Disorder.
- Discussed treatment goals with each client and created an individualized treatment plan.
- Tracked client progress with notes in a computer database while maintaining client confidentiality.
- Participated in treatment team meetings consisting of social workers, a psychiatrist, and several clinical counselors to gain clinical suggestions on the best methods for assisting clients to progress in treatment.

VOLUNTEER EXPERIENCE

Victim Advocate, United Way of Mississippi, Biloxi, MS   June 2009 – May 2010
- Answered incoming calls on a hotline for victims of abuse and referred calls to law enforcement as needed.
- Provided crisis support to victims and received training to de-escalate situations and calm callers.

Career Coach, Veterans Inc., Biloxi, MS   May 2009 – September 2009
- Conducted intake interviews with veteran clients who were seeking employment assistance.
- Discussed potential career options based on the client's skills, employment experience, and education.

Mental Health Counseling Page 2

PROJECT & CHANGE MANAGEMENT

Houston, TX 77001 | email@email.com | (555) 555-5555

SUMMARY OF QUALIFICATIONS

U.S. Navy veteran and project manager with a PMP certification, a Master's in Management and Leadership and experience in the strategic planning, facilitation, and management of high-impact projects. Proven track record in analyzing processes and applying lean methodologies to determine inefficiencies and develop improvements. Experienced in dropping production costs without sacrificing safety or employee morale while achieving high revenue growth. Regularly supervise cross-functional teams, delegating assignments, monitoring progress, providing performance evaluations, and identifying professional development opportunities. Experienced in managing a $3 million budget, maintaining equipment inventories, and integrating new technologies to improve productivity. Regularly analyze sensitive documents, compiling data into reports for executive management.

CORE COMPETENCIES

Change Management | Process Improvement | Data Analysis | Strategic Planning | Organizational Development
Technology Integration | Lean Methods | Policy Development | Inventory & Resource Management

EDUCATION & SPECIALIZED TRAINING

Project Management Professional (PMP), Project Management Institute, Issued: June 2017

Master of Science, Management & Leadership, University of Houston, Houston, TX, May 2016

Bachelor of Science, Business Administration, University of Tennessee, Knoxville, TN, May 2007

PROFESSIONAL EXPERIENCE

Project Management Consultant   June 2016 – January 2020
Houston Consulting Group, Houston, TX

- Assessed organizational processes, procedures, policies, and employee productivity to identify areas of improvement and deliver an exponential return on investment (ROI) for client companies.
- Assisted a manufacturing client in improving organizational safety from 12 accidents per month to achieve zero accidents per year by updating safety policies and creating employee safety training.
- Created an onboarding training program for employment specialists within a nonprofit organization which resulted in an immediate increase in connecting clients to desired employment.
- Selected by executive management to update the organization's internal process for assigning projects to consultants which boosted morale and led to a drop in consultant turnover.

Organizational Change Management Consultant (Contract)   March 2014 – June 2016
Stellar Shoes Inc., Houston, TX

- Created and implemented change management strategies to maximize the participation of over 1,500 employees during a transition from physical stores locations to an eBusiness model.
- Conducted impact analyses, assessing change readiness and identifying key stakeholders across the entire organization.
- Coached senior leaders and executives in the best methods for acting as change sponsors and facilitated open table discussions between leaders and their staff to boost morale.
- Implemented a pre and post-transition employee survey which gave staff the opportunity to provide their input pre-transition and showed a 20% increase in employee satisfaction post-transition.
- Developed a staff training program with input from the top 10 employees to streamline the transition to an eBusiness platform with minimal employee turnover.

Project Manager Page 1

Employment Program Director   June 2011 – February 2014
Hire More Vets, Dallas, TX
- Directed and coordinated a veteran employment program which assisted over 350 local veterans to connect with employment opportunities.
- Supervised 14 career services personnel and 3 coordinators across 13 locations, assigning individual performance metrics to staff which aligned with the organization's overall goals.
- Conducted bi-annual performance evaluations to improve individual performance, identifying areas in need of improvement, suggesting future training opportunities, and fostering career development.
- Regularly met with executives to provide program updates and present quarterly budget forecasts.
- Completed quarterly program analyses to assess program impact, identify opportunities for improvement, and pivot program strategies to be more effective in connecting veterans to employment.
- Managed a $2 million program budget which included employee payroll, regional career fairs, staff travel, and financial assistance for veterans.

Shipping & Distribution Manager   June 2007 – June 2011
Bits & Bobs, Dallas, TX
- Managed inventory control for specialized equipment, supplies, and materials, conducting periodic inspections to mitigate property loss and identify any defective equipment.
- Spearheaded the complete overhaul of the organization's warehouse layout to maximize shipping efficiency and transitioned to SAP technology which boosted productivity by 35%.
- Communicated with personnel at all organizational levels and collaborated with commercial vendors to ensure the timely completion of projects.
- Saved the organization $2 million in labor hours by strategically organizing contract service deliveries.

Professional Experience Continued:

- **Intelligence Manager**, U.S. Navy, Various Locations, January 2004 – May 2007
- **Intelligence Trainer & Supervisor**, U.S. Navy, Various Locations, June 2000 – January 2004
- **Data Analyst**, U.S. Navy, Various Locations, April 1998 – June 2000

AFFILIATIONS & MEMBERSHIPS

- Member, The Association of Project Managers, June 2017 – Present
- Board Member, Wounded Warrior Project, May 2018 – May 2019
- President, Veterans Employment Initiative of Houston, February 2017 – February 2018; Member: January 2012 – Present
- Community Engagement Coordinator, Team Red, White, and Blue Dallas Chapter, June 2011 – February 2014

Project Manager Page 2

Recreational Therapist

Fayetteville, NC 28309 | 555.555.5555 | email@email.com

SUMMARY OF QUALIFICATIONS

Certified recreational therapist with over 9 of experience in recreation management and adaptive sports at U.S. military installations. Proven track record in the planning and implementation of therapeutic services and events for wounded military members utilizing outdoor recreation programs as the therapeutic modality. Regularly performed therapeutic assessments to determine each client's abilities before creating goals and objectives or refining services to meet client's therapeutic needs. Experienced in creating and growing all new outdoor recreation therapy programs to meet client's needs. Possess a Bachelor's in Recreation and Leisure Services.

CORE COMPETENCIES

Recreation Therapy | Program Management | Supervision & Instruction | Customer Service | Adaptive Sports Budgeting | Facility Management | Equipment Inventory & Maintenance | Staff & Volunteer Management

EMPLOYMENT EXPERIENCE

Military Adaptive Sports Coordinator   December 2016 – January 2019
Navy Wounded Warrior Safe Harbor Program, Washington Navy Yard, DC

- Facilitated adapted sports and reconditioning programs and activities for recovering Navy and Coast Guard Wounded Warriors.
- Assisted service members with registering and attending local community activities and events.
- Provided multiple adaptive sport camps and training camps for competitions such as the Warrior Games and the Invictus Games which included various programming and adaptive sports.
- Participated in DoD Military Adaptive Sports & Reconditioning team decisions that impacted programming and operations.

Parks & Recreation Supervisor   January 2014 – December 2016
City of Ashville Parks & Recreation, Ashville, NC

- Established and provided recreation and sports programs, after-school programs, adaptive programming, military adaptive sports programs, senior activities, fitness programs, and seasonal activities.
- Supervised, scheduled, and assigned daily tasks for 8 part-time employees, additional seasonal staff, volunteers, and college intern students.
- Provided multiple adaptive sports and activities to include wheelchair basketball and archery in coordination with the local Military Adaptive Sports Program from Fort Bragg.
- Managed the appropriate staffing for 3 gymnasiums, 2 pools, and 4 multi-use rooms, coordinating the daily, weekly, and monthly schedules for all building activities and classes.
- Conducted quarterly facility inspections, identifying any building safety issues and scheduling and budgeting for maintenance as needed.

Supervisory Recreation Specialist & Outdoor Recreation Manager   September 2011 – January 2014
MWR Sigonella Naval Air Station, Sicily, Italy

- Managed the Information, Tickets, and Tours program and Outdoor Recreation to include cultural tours, adventure programs, local attraction sales, park and pavilion rentals, and rental equipment checkout.
- Supervised 9 employees, assigning daily tasks, maintaining timekeeping and payroll, providing yearly appraisals, and conducting corrective counselings.
- Trained 22 personnel and volunteers in program facilitation and ensured adherence to all safety policies.
- Packaged, developed, and directed tours and programs to meet community needs including offering a variety of local Sicilian tours and mainland Italy tours.

Recreation Therapist Page 1

Outdoor Recreation Director   April 2008 – September 2011
MWR Fort Bragg Outdoor Recreation, Fort Bragg, NC
- Directed the staffing, programing, and facilitation of all outdoor recreation departments and supervised over 45 personnel including 5 full-time facility managers and 40 part-time and flex time staff members.
- Managed personnel actions such as hiring, time keeping, payroll processing, performance appraisals, corrective counselings, and termination of employment.
- Continuously evaluated the effectiveness of all programs and activities within Outdoor Recreation to ensure customer's needs were met.
- Assisted in the planning and facilitation of therapeutic programs and events with the Warrior Transition Unit including horseback riding, biking, archery, challenge course programs, and special events.

Recreation Specialist & Programs Manager   June 2006 – April 2008
MWR Fort Bragg Outdoor Recreation, Fort Bragg, NC
- Created and implemented Fort Bragg's Outdoor Recreation Adventure Programs including weekly Adventure Trips, Therapeutic Programs, and Challenge Course Complex programs.
- Supervised 3 managers, 6 employees, and multiple volunteers delegating daily tasks, conducting performance evaluations, and making decisions on hiring, termination, and disciplinary actions.
- Responsible for the planning, scheduling, coordination, and implementation of all adventure programs, activities, and events including the creation and facilitation of a therapeutic horseback riding program.
- Developed initial program guidelines, ensuring all programs met industry standards and safety policies.

EDUCATION AND CERTIFICATION

- **Bachelor of Science, Recreation & Leisure Services** with a focus in Therapeutic Recreation and Outdoor Recreation, Middle Tennessee State University, Murfreesboro, TN, May 2006
- **Certified Therapeutic Recreation Specialist (CTRS)**, National Council for Therapeutic Recreation Certification, NCTRC, New York, NY, Issued: May 2006

Recreation Therapist Page 2

REGISTERED NURSE (RN)

Jefferson City, TN 37760 | 555-555-5555 | email@email.com

SUMMARY OF QUALIFICATIONS

Registered nurse licensed to practice in TN with a Bachelor of Science in Nursing (BSN) and over 4 years of experience as an RN and 6 years as a Licensed Practical Nurse. Proven track record in conducting clinical assessments and evaluations, identifying and treating patient's physiological issues or communicating patient's issues to on-site physician. Regularly supervise LPN's and CNA's, assigning caseloads, delegating tasks, and providing assistance as needed to ensure top-quality patient care. Experienced in creating and updating clinical notes in an electronic medical records database while adhering to all HIPAA and privacy regulations.

KEY SKILLS

Clinical Assessments & Evaluations | Quality Patient Care | Medical Records Management | Patient Safety
Medication Administration | Medical Team Collaboration | Individual Treatment Plans | Patient Confidentiality

PROFESSIONAL EXPERIENCE

Labor & Deliver Nurse (RN)   May 2016 – Present
Center for Women, UT Medical Center, Knoxville, TN

- Provide direct patient care to an assigned group of labor and delivery patients, prioritizing the delivery of care using time and resources efficiently while providing quality patient services during interactions.
- Assess each patient's physical and mental health by observing patient interactions with their significant other to determine patient's educational, physiological, psychosocial, comfort, and safety needs.
- Plan and coordinate care and follow-up with other associates, departments, physicians, and healthcare administration management staff.
- Evaluate and document any changes in patient's healthcare status and communicate symptomatology and results of diagnostic studies with physicians.

Licensed Practical Nurse (LPN)   June 2010 – May 2016
Country Living Retirement Center, White Pine, TN

- Directed and supervised the daily work assignments of resident care associates (CNA's) to ensure all 35 residents received adequate care at their individual level of need.
- Administered medications and evaluated residents' issues or medical concerns, discussing issues with the resident, their family members, and the resident's medical doctor as appropriate.
- Applied understanding of pathophysiological and psychosocial changes associated with the aging process and developed a music and dance program for residents which increased physical mobility.
- Assisted in the development and revision of resident service plans as per state regulatory requirements.

Certified Nursing Assistant (CNA)   January 2007 – June 2010
Volunteers of America Residential Center, Dandridge, TN

- Assisted resident clients in completing activities of daily living (ADL's) while ensuring all interactions were pleasant and professional.
- Maintained detailed documentation regarding client progress toward individual treatment goals.
- Administered client medications in accordance with physician's orders and tracked administration or medication refusal in each client's record using an electronic medical records database.
- Operated a company vehicle to transport clients to appointments or local community activities.

EDUCATION & LICENSURE

- Registered Nurse (RN) License, TN Board of Nursing, Issued: May 2016
- Licensed Practical Nurse (LPN), TN Board of Nursing, Issued: May 2010
- Bachelor of Science in Nursing (BSN), University of Tennessee, Knoxville, TN, May 2010

Registered Nurse

Restaurant Manager

Nashville, TN 37116 ♦ 555-555-5555 ♦ Email@email.com

SUMMARY OF QUALIFICATIONS

Restaurant manager with over 8 years of training, supervision, and management experience in the food service industry. Proven track record in maintaining the cleanliness of commercial kitchen equipment and appliances, food preparation surfaces, and consumable product storage areas. Regularly interviewed, hired, and trained incoming employees, including servers and kitchen staff, to provide a quality customer interaction for all guests. Experienced the inventory management of perishable food supplies, conducting periodic inspections to remove expired items and create monthly orders. Able to communicate with external agencies to develop collaborative partnerships that drive sales. Possess a Bachelor's degree and a Food Safety Manager certification.

CORE COMPETENCIES

Supervision & Training ♦ Recruiting & Hiring ♦ Customer Service ♦ Promotions & Sales ♦ FDA Regulations
Inventory & Supply Management ♦ Equipment Maintenance ♦ Scheduling & Payroll ♦ Facilities Management

EDUCATION & CERTIFICATIONS

- Bachelor of Arts, Business Management, University of Tennessee, Knoxville, TN, December 2012
- Tennessee Food Safety Manager Certification, American National Standards Institute, June 2013
- Tennessee Food Safety Handlers Certification, American National Standards Institute, May 2011

PROFESSIONAL EXPERIENCE

Food Service Manager I   June 2018 – Present
Dining Services, Tennessee State University, Nashville, TN
- Manage over 45 student employees and 25 union and non-union personnel, delegating daily, weekly, and monthly tasks to provide food services to over 3,000 diners on a daily basis.
- Directly supervise personnel, providing performance evaluations, conducting corrective counseling or disciplinary actions as necessary, and providing opportunities for professional development.
- Conduct interviews, hire staff, and facilitate new employee training to ensure understanding and adherence to industry safety regulations and organizational policies.
- Communicate with patrons regarding food allergies or medical issues while maintaining confidentiality.
- Review policies and procedures to identify, develop, and implement more effective methods which directly resulted in a 20% improvement across kitchen staff efficiency without jeopardizing food safety.

Store Manager   January 2015 – May 2018
Tom's Pizza, Nashville, TN
- Managed the daily functioning of a fast food pizza restaurant which earned $400,000 over the yearly sales expectation for 2017 and was on track to surpass that in 2018.
- Interviewed, hired, and managed kitchen and front staff employees, creating weekly schedules and recording hours worked in order to process pay.
- Inventoried products, removing expired items and ordering replacement or specialty products.
- Prepared food such as sandwiches, salads, and pizzas using safety precautions and sanitary measures.
- Communicated with customers regarding orders, comments, and/or complaints in order to identify possible resolutions and maintain customer satisfaction.
- Cleaned and organized dining, kitchen, and service areas and trained staff in appropriate food preparation methods and policies.

Restaurant Manager Page 1

Assistant Manager   December 2012 – December 2014
Carrabba's Italian Grill, Knoxville, TN
- Assisted in hiring and training over 20 front house staff members before the opening of a new location.
- Maintained a clean and inviting dining area and providing weekly training to servers regarding specials and promotions in order to drive sales.
- Developed a partnership with several local breweries to carry their flagship beers on tap, collaborating with the head chef to create a menu and pair each beer with a specialty menu item.
- Created weekly staff schedules, monitored hours worked, and entered data into a payroll system.

Server   May 2011 – December 2012
Cheddars, Knoxville, TN
- Greeted restaurant patrons, answering any questions regarding menu items, making recommendations, and receiving orders while maintaining attention to detail to ensure the appropriate meals were prepared.
- Provided friendly and timely customer service, exceeding the expectations of restaurant patrons.
- Interfaced with proprietary computer systems to communicate orders to kitchen staff, create order totals at the end of the meal, and process cash or credit transactions.
- Maintained a clean dining area and assisted teammates in completing any extra tasks as needed.

Restaurant Manager Page 2

Sales Manager

Los Angeles, CA 90013 ♦ 555-555-5555 ♦ email@email.com ♦ LinkedIn Profile Link

SUMMARY OF QUALIFICATIONS

Sales team manager with a Bachelor's degree in Business Administration and experience in software and retail sales. Proven track record in analyzing system processes and procedures to improve productivity, decrease costs, increase revenue, or maximize system capabilities. Experienced in managing 12 sales personnel, providing sales training, conducting performance evaluations, and ensuring all individuals met assigned sales goals. Regularly analyze market trends, identifying consumer preferences and competitors' strategies to create high-impact sales strategies. Experienced in collaborating with other departments in order to fully understand and convey product capabilities and highlights. Possess the certification for Professional Sales Person (CPSP).

CORE COMPETENCIES

Sales Team Management ♦ Data-Driven Strategies ♦ Consumer Research ♦ B2B Sales ♦ KPI Metrics
Sales Training ♦ Product Launches ♦ Partnership Development ♦ Sales Funnels ♦ Supervision & Instruction

PROFESSIONAL EXPERIENCE

Sales Manager   July 2018 – January 2020
Star Power Shoes, Los Angeles, CA
- Recruited, interviewed, and hired 15 commission-based sales representatives, conducting staff training in product lines, sales highlights, and promotional launches.
- Assisted the Marketing & Sales Director in developing quarterly staff sales metrics and provided one-on-one retraining for sales representatives who fell short of their assigned goals.
- Developed online sales funnels and built partnerships with physical shoe stores, gaining top product placement with front window displays in over 300 stores which earned $600,000 in first year's sales.
- Collaborated closely with the marketing team on all major product launches to ensure sales success.
- Reviewed weekly accounts receivables to ensure the receipt of payment for the products shipped.

Global Account (Sales) Executive   July 2015 – May 2018
Easy Compute, Los Angeles, CA
- Collaborated with a sales team of marketing and social media specialists to monitor corporate software purchasing trends and communicated with software engineers to gain full understanding of product uses.
- Developed strategic plans to increase sales opportunities in assigned territories and promote continual revenue growth.
- Exceeded 2016 sales goal by 8% and developed a sales referral program in 2017 which boosted sales to 25% over performance expectations.
- Selected by management to train and mentor incoming sales representatives and provide training on the successful sales referral program to all existing sales representatives.

Sales Representative   September 2013 – April 2015
Clothing Rack, Los Angeles, CA
- Answered customer questions in a high-end boutique clothing store and provided assistance in locating clothing in specific styles or colors as well as matching accessories.
- Used hand-held scanners and a computer system to track product inventory and enter information into a computerized database.
- Processed sales transactions or product returns while providing a positive customer experience and boosted store sales 5% by asking all customers if they'd considered an accessory for their new outfit.
- Trained and mentored incoming sales representatives to provide exceptional customer service and follow all store policies and procedures.

Sales Manager Page 1

Outreach Consultant   October 2009 – September 2013
LA Housing Services, Los Angeles, CA

- Planned and organized events such as service fairs, conferences, or seminars to spread program awareness and increase program enrollment.
- Collaborated with stakeholders including banks, churches, community organizations, local businesses, and state or local government agencies.
- Created and implemented various service improvement initiatives such as the intake process to increase the organization's productivity and client satisfaction rates.
- Developed a comprehensive marketing plan with targeted outreach strategies to attract new clients.
- Managed the organization's online presence and created social media accounts with daily content to build organizational and program awareness.

EDUCATION & SPECIALIZED TRAINING

- Bachelor of Arts, Business Administration, Angeles College, Los Angeles, CA, May 2015
- Certified Professional Sales Person (CPSP), National Association of Sales Professionals, May 2015

Sales Manager Page 2

SECURITY GUARD

Phoenix, AZ, 86336 | 555-555-5555 | email@email.com

SUMMARY OF QUALIFICATIONS

Licensed security guard with an Associate's in Criminal Justice and over 8 years of experience securing buildings, personnel, and prisoners. Proven track record in deescalating hostile situations while providing a quality customer service experience to both internal and external customers. Experienced in identifying process or policy inefficiencies and implementing improvements to increase safety and efficiency. Regularly create and maintain official documentation in an electronic database. Able to communicate with external agencies to build collaborative relationships and increase security. Possess a driver's license and certified in CPR and First Aid.

KEY SKILLS

Building & Site Security | Prison Security | Safety Policies | Documentation & Reports | Communication
Process Improvement | Customer Service | Inventory & Maintenance | CCTV | Relationship Development

PROFESSIONAL EXPERIENCE

Security Officer   May 2016 – January 2020
Arizona State Prison, Phoenix, AZ

- Provided security to several areas of a state prison and ensured the safety of all staff and prisoners.
- Assisted in the development of new prisoner transport procedures which decreased prisoner infractions and minimized the potential for escape.
- Communicated clearly with security staff, onsite counselors, and medical staff to provide information regarding prisoner health and convey any safety issues prisoners might pose.
- Regularly called upon by senior officers to deescalate tense or hostile situations with prisoners.
- Created, updated, and maintained documentation regarding prisoner wellness, noting infractions, issues with other prisoners, or suspected gang relations.

Prisoner Transport Guard   April 2015 – May 2016
Guard of Arizona LLC, Phoenix, AZ

- Securely transported prisoners between prisons, county jails, courthouses, and hospitals.
- Operated and maintained a company passenger van in accordance with all regulations.
- Recorded and maintained mileage logs via an electronic database and documented any issues, irregularities, or prisoner infractions occurring during transport operations.
- Properly secured prisoners during transport to ensure their own safety as well as staff safety.

Armed Security Guard   September 2012 – April 2015
Benton Health Headquarters, Phoenix, AZ

- Created a new visitor check-in policy which decreased unexpected office visits and increased the safety of all company personnel by limiting building access only to expected visitors.
- Provided a quality customer service experience to all visitors while verifying identification and determining their destination within the building.
- Regularly deescalated situations involving difficult and occasionally hostile visitors and was lauded by executive leadership for successfully demobilizing a physically violent guest before harm came to staff.
- Developed dialogue with local police and fire departments and collaborated to create emergency plans.

EDUCATION & SPECIALIZED TRAINING

- Associate of Arts, Criminal Justice, Arizona State University, Tempe, AZ, May 2016
- Armed Security Guard License, AZ Department of Public Safety, Issued: May 2012
- Arizona Guard Card Training, Security Guard Services, Glendale, AZ, April 2012
- CPR & First Aid, American Heart Association, Expires: January 2022

Security Guard

Senior Paralegal

Nashville, TN 37115 ♦ email@email.com ♦ 555-555-5555

SUMMARY OF QUALIFICATIONS

Senior paralegal with a Bachelor's in Legal Studies and experience in law offices specializing in litigation. Proven track record in supervising case management for up to 5 paralegals and legal secretaries to ensure the appropriate handling of clients and case materials for federal and state courts. Regularly created, updated, organized, and maintained official documents or sensitive case files in secure databases. Experienced in office management, conducting inventory and ordering supplies, facilitating smooth daily office operations, and providing bookkeeping services such as account management, billing, and reconciliations. Possess a Paralegal Certificate.

CORE COMPETENCIES

Legal Research ♦ Administration & Scheduling ♦ Calendar Management ♦ Case Filings & Documents
Case Management ♦ Quality Client Services ♦ Billing & Bookkeeping ♦ Legal Policy ♦ Inventory Management

PROFESSIONAL EXPERIENCE

Senior Paralegal & Bookkeeper   November 2016 – Present
We Win Law Office, Nashville, TN

- Incorporated a new calendar management software system with accountability for managing and coordinating all appointments for 7 lawyers and 5 paralegals.
- Scheduled, coordinated, and managed conferences, booking appropriate event spaces and creating event agendas or presentations to meet management's expectations.
- Maintained client accounting files, reconciling client accounts, collecting payments, and utilizing QuickBooks to reconcile bank accounts, prepare payrolls, pay bills, and prepare tax information.
- Managed all office facilities, coordinating repairs and paying bills such as the lease, electricity, or water.
- Reviewed client documents and case files to prepare comprehensive reports for hearings and trials.
- Drafted pleadings and authored professional correspondence for internal and external distribution.
- Managed the inventory of office supplies, conducting counts to mitigate asset loss, ensuring appropriate supply levels were on hand, and ordering new items to support the law firm's daily processes.

Paralegal   June 2012 – October 2016
John & Jane Law Office, Knoxville, TN

- Conducted client intake processes, gathering client information and scheduling follow up meeting as necessary while providing a quality customer service experience for each client.
- Prepared exhibits, presentations, and briefs to be used by lawyers in depositions or trials.
- Assisted attorneys in preparing for trials, hearings, and depositions, conducting background and social media checks on parties and witnesses and requesting medical or police records as needed.
- Converted the entire office to a paperless system and regularly created, reviewed, processed, and organized official legal documents, case filings, client files, pleadings, orders, and motions.

Administrative Assistant
Morgan Stanley, Knoxville, TN

- Managed calendars, scheduled meetings, and set up conferences in offices across the state.
- Assisted team members in monitoring their email and sorted mail to appropriate team members.
- Answered incoming phone calls, providing information or transferring callers to other departments.
- Created, updated, and maintained both electronic and hardcopy documents.

EDUCATION & CERTIFICATIONS

Bachelor of Science, Legal Studies, University of Tennessee, Knoxville, TN, May 2012

Certified Paralegal, National Association of Legal Assistants (NALA), Expires: June 2021

Senior Paralegal

Social Media Coordinator

Chicago, IL 60176 ♦ 555-555-5555 ♦ email@email.com ♦ LinkedIn Profile Link

SUMMARY OF QUALIFICATIONS

Digital marketing and social media coordinator with a Bachelor's degree in Communications and experience in creating marketing strategies that successfully reach a target market and convert to sales. Proven track record in increasing lead generation by creating engaging content on the most appropriate social media platforms for target market. Regularly run concurrent social media campaigns and contract with top influencers to build brand or product awareness. Experienced in communicating across internal departments and collaborating with external individuals or agencies to build mutually beneficial partnerships. Regularly manage the curation and use of user-generated content for high-impact product launches and social media campaigns.

CORE COMPETENCIES

Social Media Campaigns ♦ Data Analysis ♦ Content Optimization ♦ User-Generated Content Management
SEO/SEM ♦ Partnership Development ♦ Product Launches ♦ Influencer Collaboration ♦ Metrics

EDUCATION & SPECIALIZED TRAINING

- Digital Social & Selling Specialist Certification, Digital Marketing Institute, August 2019
- Facebook Blueprint Certification, Facebook, July 2018
- Google Analytics IQ Certification, Google Analytics Academy, May 2018
- Social Media Manager Certification, Management & Strategy Institute, April 2016
- Bachelor of Arts, Communications, University of Illinois at Chicago, Chicago, IL, May 2013

PROFESSIONAL EXPERIENCE

Social Media Coordinator   June 2017 – December 2019
Solo Sweatz, Chicago, IL
- Collaborated with the marketing and sales team to develop a strategic plan for building product and brand awareness among the target market customers before the first product was launched.
- Led content organization, optimization, curation, and approval workflows within an internal tool used to manage user-generated content.
- Developed concurrent campaigns across social media sites in collaboration with 12 health and fitness influencers for the first product launch which resulted in over $1 million in the first week of sales.
- Trained 5 customer service representatives who responded to customer's comments on social media.
- Developed a company presence on the athletically related social media platforms Strava and Fitbit, leading to over 700 followers collectively across both sites.

Digital Marketing & Content Coordinator   July 2015– May 2017
Long Life Health, Chicago, IL
- Created engaging content for social media, websites, and blog posts which increased company awareness and increased registration for paid online programs by 25%.
- Managed the organization's website and blog on WordPress and applied a deep understanding of SEO/SEM best practices to grow organic site visits.
- Utilized Google Analytics to assess content reach, determine the ROI of social media advertising, and develop data-driven digital marketing strategies to be approved by the marketing manager.
- In a collaborative project with the HR department, assisted senior executives to create or update their LinkedIn profiles to funnel top talent to the company's open positions.

Social Media Coordinator Page 1

Social Media Specialist   June 2013 – July 2015
Your Money Our Problem Co., Chicago, IL
- Gained customer feedback through a digital survey and applied the information to the total redesign of all email marketing content which led to a 12% boost in click-through rates.
- Wrote compelling, on-brand social media content across a variety of digital channels such as social media, blogs, the company website, and email and curated attached photos to reinforce the written word.
- Scheduled social media posts during the highest-traffic periods for each platform and created social media campaigns.
- Updated SEO on the company website and immediately saw a 10% boost in site visitors.

Social Media Marketing Intern   May 2012 – May 2013
University of Illinois, Chicago, IL
- Collaborated with the communications and marketing department to craft and design content for a newly formed graduate school program in order to increase lead generation of potential students.
- Assisted in developing a comprehensive strategy to drive new email database growth of University Alumni using content marketing.
- Managed content creation and all official responses for the Communication Department's social media accounts on Twitter, Facebook, Instagram, and LinkedIn.

Social Media Coordinator Page 2

Teacher

Billings, MT 59102 ♦ 555-555-5555 ♦ Email@email.com

SUMMARY OF QUALIFICATIONS

Licensed teacher with a Master's in Education and over 12 years of experience instructing elementary and high school-age children. Proven track record in creating engaging and data-driven lesson plans to facilitate a continued student interest in the life-long learning process. Regularly grade papers, homework, and special projects, maintaining grades in an electronic database. Experienced in working with children with special needs or behavioral issues and maintaining order within the classroom. Regularly create a safe and inclusive classroom environment to foster more engaged learning.

CORE COMPETENCIES

Data-Driven Strategies ♦ Lesson Plan Creation ♦ Math & English Instruction ♦ Parent Communication
Classroom Safety ♦ Inventory & Supply Management ♦ Evaluation & Grading ♦ Collaboration

PROFESSIONAL EXPERIENCE

Elementary School Teacher   June 2013 – Present
Friendship Public Charter School, Billings, MT
- Create and facilitate engaging lesson plans at the appropriate grade level for a 4th grade classroom with 26-30 students while addressing a full range of student needs and learning styles.
- Foster a safe environment conducive to learning and asking questions without fear of being wrong.
- Closely communicate with parents or guardians to promote parent involvement and ensure students receive continual learning support at home.
- Attend teaching workshops and conferences to learn about new classroom technologies or teaching strategies and incorporate new information into a yearly lesson plan review to make improvements.
- Maintain documentation regarding student grades in an electronic database and meet all school deadlines for grading.

Elementary School Teacher   September 2010 – May 2013
Hawthorne Elementary School, Missoula, MT
- Planned and executed engaging activities and lessons for a 3rd grade classroom of 22 students.
- Instructed students individually and in group settings using various teaching methods within a safe learning environment.
- Created and maintained administrative documentation regarding student grades and behavior and provided weekly parent updates regarding their child's progress and difficulties.
- Established and enforced guidelines and procedures for maintaining order within the classroom.
- Provided instruction for a special needs student and several students with behavioral issues.
- Planned, coordinated, and facilitated educational field trips in collaboration with several other elementary school teachers.

Teacher's Assistant   August 2008 – August 2010
Big Sky High School, Missoula, MT
- Supervised 10-12 students in an in-school-suspension classroom, providing a safe and secure environment for all students.
- Identified students struggling with lessons and modified teaching strategies to ensure student comprehension.
- Communicated with the assistant principal and teachers regarding each student's behavior.
- Documented daily tardy occurrences, behavioral issues, and student attendance.

Teacher Page 1

Substitute Teacher   June 2004 – August 2008
Big Sky High School & Hawthorne Elementary School, Missoula, MT
- Provided substitute teaching for high school and elementary school students on an as needed basis.
- Implemented lesson plans, directed students in completing classwork, and assigned homework as appropriate to lessons.
- Maintained control of the classroom at all times and created daily reports for the classroom teacher.

LICENSE & EDUCATION

- Master of Arts, Education, University of Montana, Missoula, MT, May 2007
- Bachelor of Arts, Elementary Education, University of Montana, Missoula, MT, May 2004
- Class I Professional Teaching License, Montana Office of Public Instruction, Helena, MT, May 2010

Teacher Page 2

WAREHOUSE ASSOCIATE

Tacoma, WA 98406 | 555-555-5555 | email@email.com

SUMMARY OF QUALIFICATIONS

Warehouse associate with over 8 years of experience picking and packing products to fulfill customer orders. Proven track record in identifying shipping or warehouse picking inefficiencies and developing more effective methods to improve packing speed or increase customer satisfaction. Experienced in conducting full-scale warehouse product inventories to ensure products match system records. Regularly provide a quality customer service experience in person or over the phone. Experienced in the safe use of a fork-lift to load and unload product shipments. Able to communicate clearly and currently completing a Bachelor's in Business Administration.

KEY SKILLS

Shipping & Distribution | Securing Shipments | Quality Customer Service | Documentation & Reports
Inventory Management | CRM Systems | Picking & Packing | Order Fulfillment | Site Safety

PROFESSIONAL EXPERIENCE

Order Fulfillment Technician   May 2016 – January 2020
Pick & Pack, Puyallup, WA

- Reviewed customer orders in a Customer Relationship Management (CRM) system and picked products from the warehouse to fulfill customer requests.
- Utilized an RF handheld scanner while picking to assign products into specific customer orders.
- Suggested a more efficient method for packing a popular fragile item to decrease the likelihood of the product being damaged during the shipping process and decreased customer product complaints.
- Selected to assist the manager in conducting periodic inventory assessments on over $10 million worth of warehouse products to ensure inventory matched electronic records.

Warehouse Worker   April 2012 – May 2016
Smiley Distribution Center, Monaca, PA

- Constructed boxes of varying sizes in relation to the types of products being shipped and ensured all products were carefully packed in order to eliminate or minimize damages to products.
- Used a fork-lift to load outgoing shipments into large cargo shipping containers, semi-trucks, and box trucks while adhering to all shipping regulations, weight restrictions, and organizational policies.
- Developed a positive relationship with delivery truck drivers, identifying a driver complaint with the loading process and developing a better method to organize shipments for more effective deliveries.
- Reviewed and processed customer invoices and called customers as needed to resolve any issues with product delivery times or missing items.

Delivery Driver   September 2010 – April 2012
Quick Delivery LLC, Pittsburgh, PA

- Operated a company box truck to complete wholesale, retail, and residential deliveries from a local distribution center.
- Reviewed all shipping manifests during the warehouse loading procedure to ensure accurate shipments.
- Provided a quality customer service experience during all deliveries as well as over the phone when responding to any customer complaints.
- Received employee of the month 2 times during tenure for providing fast deliveries with no accidents.

EDUCATION

- (Currently) Associate of Arts, Business Administration, Bates Technical College, Tacoma, WA, Estimated Graduation: December 2022
- Fork Life Certification, Smiley Distribution Center, Monaca, PA, May 2012

Warehouse Technician

About the Author

Jennifer Jelliff-Russell has been helping job seekers discover the flaws in their job search approach for over seven years and has assisted clients from a variety of industries at all organizational levels. Her educational background in Psychology with a Master's in Community Counseling was the perfect base upon which to build a career in employment services and coaching as it honed the skills needed to listen attentively and identify each client's job search mistakes. Jennifer especially enjoys assisting professionals in transition including veterans transitioning to civilian employment and women professionals navigating the leap to management. She is also a speaker on women's professional development for corporations and conferences. Learn more about her career services at www.evergrowthcoach.com and subscribe for free career coaching materials at https://www.evergrowthcoach.com/subscribe-landing.

www.ingramcontent.com/pod-product-compliance
Lightning Source LLC
Chambersburg PA
CBHW080713050426

42336CB00062B/3228